IPAD 11 USER GUIDE

for Seniors

Step-by-Step Beginners Manual on How to Setup and use the 11th Generation iPad (2025 A16) with iPadOS 18 Tips and Tricks

Ellie Mannus

TABLE OF CONTENTS

CHAPTER 4: PERSONALIZE YOUR IPAD
..122

CHAPTER 5: MASTERING TEXT INPUT ON IPAD..178

CHAPTER 6: BOOKS 229

CHAPTER 8: SEAMLESSLY CONNECT WITH EVERYONE: HOW TO INITIATE A GROUP FACETIME CALL ON YOUR IPAD

CHAPTER 1: INTRODUCTION TO IPAD 11

IPAD 11 PARTS

Below is a deeper explanation of all the various parts on the iPad 11, their function, and how they will relate to you in using your iPad, whether it be for communications, media consumption, or productivity.

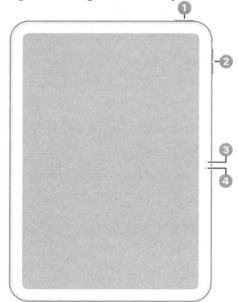

1. Top Button/Touch ID

The top button on the iPad 11 has two easy actions that it does: it turns the device on and off and it locks with Touch ID.

    1. On/Off Power: You will press and hold the top button until it powers on. To power it off, hold the button down until the "slide to power off" screen shows up and then swipe to turn it off.

2. Touch ID: The top button also includes a fingerprint sensor that allows you to unlock the iPad securely with your fingerprint. You can enroll multiple fingerprints in the settings, so your finger becomes a fast and sure "key" for access-somewhat like unlocking a door with a real key.

Certainly, this makes the top button vital to security and basic operation, doing just about everything-from buying apps to signing into services-easy with one touch.

2. Volume Buttons

The iPad 11 has two volume buttons that sit on its side; they let you quickly change your volume.

1. Volume Up: The top button is used for increasing the volume of your media, such as music, videos, or alerts.
2. Volume Down: The bottom button is used to lessen the volume.

These buttons are similar in concept to a volume rotary on a speaker or on a remote of a television; they're easy to reach to immediately adjust the volume. You can also quickly mute your device by holding down the volume-down button. These buttons interact with software functions, which means you could also adjust the volume using the Control Center or through specific applications.

3. Front Camera

The major roles of the front camera of the iPad 11 are to take selfies, for video calls, and face detection.

1. Selfies & Portraits: This is because it shoots high-quality photos and videos, supporting a feature like portrait mode that blurs the background to bring out your subject.

2. Video Calls: The major role of the front camera keeps you in view when making calls over FaceTime or other types of video conferencing.
3. Face Detection & Center Stage: Advanced technologies in this camera include face detection, ensuring it focuses on your face correctly while on calls. This same camera is used by many apps for the "Center Stage" feature, where it will also keep you within the frame-even as you're shifting around. It's almost like having your cameraman, automatically adjusting to your movements.

4. Microphone

The microphone of the iPad 11 is responsible for capturing sound while one is on calls, recording, or dictating.

1. Voice Recording & Calls: It clearly picks up your audio during FaceTime calls, video recording, or using another app like Voice Memos.
2. Dictation: It also supports speech-to-text features where you would like to dictate your messages or notes rather than typing them.

It will be very sensitive to capture your voice while canceling the background noise. Working much in the same way as most high-of-the-line camera or phone mics, the audio sounds great when speaking directly on the device or from across the room on a video call.

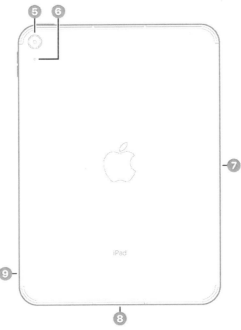

5. Rear Camera

The rear-side camera of the iPad 11 is a general-purpose tool, designed to capture high-quality photos and videos and support augmented reality experiences.

1. Photography & Videography: The rear camera of the iPad captures detailed, high-resolution images and videos. It does support auto-focus, HDR, and portrait mode for enhancing photo quality by adjusting lighting and background blur to make your subject stand out.

2. AR apps: This camera also has a critical role in AR apps. It would scan the environment to make virtual objects appear in the real world, using the iPad's screen as the interface, hence making things interactive. Bringing the digital space into your physical one.

3. Document Scanning: The back camera is also helpful to scan documents. With built-in software, it automatically detects edges of papers or receipts and takes clear images that are easily readable to save or share.

In all, the rear camera works like a professional camera with various modes in photography, video shooting capability, and a gateway to AR experiences.

6. Microphone

The new iPad 11 comes equipped with several microphones; in unison, they do a very important job of picking up sound for various purposes.

1. Recording & Sound Video Calls: These microphones come in very useful during the recording of decent sound in video shootings, voice notes, or video calls using applications such as FaceTime. Optimized to minimize the background noise, each microphone strongly focuses on your voice for crystal clear sound.

2. Siri & Dictation: The microphone also works with Siri-macOS's voice assistant that lets you instruct your computer by asking questions, setting reminders, and the like. It is equally useful to use for dictation, converting your spoken words into text as you send messages or write notes.

The microphones are finely tuned for capturing sound from various directions to make sure your voice is well-filtered in case you are recording or on calls, just as if you were using a professional external microphone on some high-of-the-range camera.

7. Smart Connector

The Smart Connector is a set of three small dots found on the side of the iPad 11, which provide direct connection access for accessories, mainly keyboards.

1. Accessories connecting: If you have an attachment like the Smart Keyboard, for example, the Smart Connector lets your attachments perform without pairing or charging. It transfers both data and power so you snap on the accessory, and it is ready for use instantly.

2. No Charging Required: This in return counteracts the original Bluetooth accessories, which had to be charged separately from your iPad. Rather, it would be a wired accessory plugged in directly from the iPad and hence hassle-free.

In other words, Smart Connector makes the iPad a bit more productive by turning it into an adept machine with seamless integration of attached accessories.

8. USB-C Connector

The USB-C port of the iPad 11 has multiple purposes: for charging, for data transfer, and to connect to other external devices.

1. Charging: This is the port utilized for charging the iPad. Via USB-C, it allows fast charging, meaning it takes less time to charge your gadget rather than using the older methods.

2. Data Transfer: You are also allowed to connect the iPad to other external devices, either a computer or an external drive, via USB-C in order to transfer files. The high speeds that can support high-speed data transfer make it suitable for transferring large files, like photos or videos, or doing backups.

3. External Devices: With the highly versatile USB-C port, it allows you to connect to a wide range of

external devices such as monitors, cameras, or audio equipment. You can connect an external display to your iPad, so both screens show the same thing, or attach a card reader to import photos directly from a camera. It acts like the hub of a computer, providing various kinds of connections and expanding the functionality of your iPad.

9. SIM Tray (Wi-Fi + Cellular)
The SIM tray houses a SIM card that you insert into the iPad for cellular services.
1. Cellular Data Connection: This includes a physical SIM card or even an eSIM in its SIM tray for Wi-Fi+Cellular iPads, which enables connections to mobile networks for internet browsing and data use when Wi-Fi is not available. You get a sort of smartphone feature to keep connected with the Internet while on the move without having to depend on Wi-Fi.
2. Roaming: You can also use the iPad outside your country, thanks to the SIM card, by connecting with other networks due to roaming services. This makes an iPad a very strong companion while on the go.

The SIM tray makes your iPad become a mobile gadget with cellular access to the network, just as your phone does on 4G or 5G.

ACCESSORIES RECOMMENDED FOR THE IPAD 11

It will now be described in some detail which functionalities and uses each iPad 11 accessory may have. All of these accessories, put together, help the iPad 11 function in a very wide variety of professional or creative settings, aside from the standard use.

1. Apple Pencil

The Apple Pencil is an extremely precise, pressure-sensitive stylus to draw on, write with, and navigate on the iPad 11.

1. Drawing & Creative Work: The Apple Pencil is fantastic for digital artists and designers, with precision rivaling conventional pencils. Equipped with the possibility to detect varying levels of pressure and tilt, you would be able to create strokes with thickness variation, shading, or details in apps such as Procreate or Adobe Fresco. It feels just like working with a high-class drawing tool and gives you immense control over your work.

2. Note-taking & Markup: Apple Pencil is very helpful for students or working professionals who take handwritten notes or like to draw and markup documents. You can write, for instance, with ease using Apple Notes or GoodNotes. It converts the handwritten text to digital form if that is what you need.

3. Navigation: The Apple Pencil can also be used to navigate the iPad, which, again, provides a more precise input than using your finger. Whether you are editing photos or working in spreadsheets, it is like a fine-pointed tool for tapping and dragging on the screen.

Magnetic attachment to the side of the iPad makes it always within reach and ready for charging and storing, a perfect companion at the behest of creativity and productivity.

2. Magic Keyboard

The Magic Keyboard is designed like a full-size keyboard with a built-in trackpad to ultimately transform the iPad 11 into something very much like a laptop.

1. Magic Keyboard-Typing Experience: Similar to using any good laptop keyboard, this device offers that tactile experience of typing. If it had backlight keys, it would be very easy to type even in low light. It is comfortable and responsive for writing long documents, emails, or even code; it turns your iPad into a powerful writing machine.

2. Trackpad: The integrated trackpad adds a completely new layer of control. To navigate, you'll be able to employ multitouch gestures-scrolling, say, or swiping between apps, or zooming-just as you would on the trackpad of a MacBook. You are practically working with the functionality of a laptop, combined into a tablet.

3. Floating Design & Adjustable Angles: The Magic Keyboard has a unique floating cantilever design and magnetically attaches to the iPad, allowing facility in adjusting the viewing angles. It is ideal for typing, drawing, or even watching media. It also keeps your iPad elevated to protect it from spills or other potential hazards.

In short, the Magic Keyboard can transform the iPad into a portable alternative to laptops by providing a professional-grade typing and navigation experience.

3. Smart Keyboard Folio

The Smart Keyboard Folio provides a protective, ultra-light case with an integrated keyboard for fast, comfortable typing on the iPad 11.

1. Typing Convenience: Weighing in at about half the weight and less in size than Apple's Magic Keyboard, the Smart Folio is still large enough to provide a very comfortable typing experience. There is no backlit keyboard or trackpad on this keyboard. Yet, it is a great tool for quickly typing out documents, sending emails, and messaging anywhere.

2. Protection & Portability: The Smart Keyboard Folio protects your iPad front and back while being slim and light, perfect for customers looking for the essential keyboard functionalities without adding heft. Think of it like a notebook cover that just so happens to double as a keyboard when you need it.

3. Easy Setup: The Smart Keyboard Folio attaches directly with the Smart Connector, making this keyboard ready for work without any charging or pairing required. Ideal for travelers who just want a no-frills typing solution.

This is ideal for those consumers who want to experience the strongest portability with minimal fuss but may want the typing facility on occasions.

4. Logitech Crayon

Logitech Crayon is an affordable, yet durable alternative to the Apple Pencil capable of executing similar functions: drawing, note taking, marking up documents, and more.

1. Precision & Tilt Sensitivity: Logitech Crayon features both pixel-perfect precision and tilt sensitivity, making it perfectly fit for drawing, coloring, or even just taking notes. It's slightly larger in diameter than that of the Apple Pencil but is designed to be more rugged, though basically processed for educational processes. Almost like using a regular crayon, with digital precision and versatility.
2. No pairing is required. One great thing about the Logitech Crayon is that, unlike the Apple Pencil, it does not require any Bluetooth pairing. You can actually just turn it on and start writing or drawing right away. It is, therefore, very user-friendly, mainly among students or for anyone who wants a no-fuss kind of gadget.
3. Compatibility & Durability: Crayon is fall resistant and can withstand day-to-day impacts, which makes it rugged for kids as well as for users who are always mobile. It also works with a wide range of iPad apps that support Apple Pencil, and delivers many of the same capabilities for a fraction of the price.

Logitech Crayon serves as a good and reliable choice for those users who want a low-budget yet functionally full stylus.

5. USB-C Hub

A USB-C hub is an essential accessory that expands the connectivity options for an iPad 11, which comes fitted with only a single USB-C port.

1. Multifunctional ports: A USB-C adapter can further facilitate various other ports such as an HDMI port, slots for SD cards, USB-A, among

many others, that make the iPad all-purpose in function. You can even attach external monitors, keyboards, and drives to it. Hence, it's like installing a number of applications on your iPad, that get you functionalities for a number of tasks.

2. File Transfer: You can transfer big files in a very short time from an external drive or memory cards via a hub, which is really helpful for a photographer or videographer who always needs to transfer photos or videos to edit. It's just about giving your iPad extra doors to connect more accessory devices at the same time.

3. Charging while connected: This feature involves many USB-C hubs that allow for pass-through charging, whereby you can charge your iPad while using all the accessories connected to it. This will be important if you're using a power-consuming accessory, like an external hard drive or another display.

More or less, the USB-C Hub turns your iPad into a productivity workstation by providing more connectivity options, hence an excellent accessory for pros or creatives with needs over and above the few ports the iPad provides.

6. Screen Protector
It serves as the thin, transparent layer stuck onto an iPad screen to provide extra defense against scratches and the like.

1. Scratch Resistance: A screen protector is mostly used for protection against scratches that result from everyday use, such as keys in your bag or incidental contact with any surface. A screen protector will keep your display looking like it just

came off the factory floor. Think of this screen protector as armor that will be protecting your iPad from minor damages to its screen.

2. Glare Reduction: Some screen protectors are anti-glare, meaning they reduce reflections from bright lights or sunlight. That is very helpful if using your iPad outdoors or in luminous environments, improving visibility and comfort.

3. These privacy screen protectors narrow the field of view such that it's just the person who is directly before the iPad sees the screen clearly. Pretty helpful in open areas-places like cafes or during public transport-so that many people cannot see the sensitive information.

In a nutshell, a screen protector is an easy and effective way to keep your iPad's display functional for as long as possible.

7. Stand for iPad

The iPad stand holds the iPad at a convenient angle for comfort over various activities.

1. Comfort Viewing: A stand allows you to position the iPad at an ergonomic angle to your neck and wrists; during extended use, such as watching videos, video calling, or reading, one either tends to crouch forward or bend towards the device. So, it is something like having a desk for the iPad itself, operating it comfortably without holding it while using it.

2. Stability: A good stand provides stability to keep the iPad from wobbling or tipping over. This is beneficial when typing or drawing, allowing for more controlled motions, similar to how having a sturdy desk enhances your productivity.

3. Versatility: Most of the stands are adjustable, which will mean you can change the height and angle depending on your preference. Whether one sits at a table or sits on the couch, an iPad stand can make the experience more personalized.

An iPad stand is among the useful accessories that would improve comfort, stability, and usability during gadget operation.

8. iPad Sleeve or Case
An iPad sleeve or case acts to ensure that the iPad remains well protected against scratches, bumps, and other elements of damage during transportation.

1. Protection: Basically, a sleeve or case is meant to protect the device from wear and tear. A sleeve that is well-padded can absorb shock from drops, while on the other hand, a rigid case can protect against scratches or dents, much like a protective shell.
2. Portability: Most of the sleeves are extremely lightweight and thin, and carrying your iPad with you in a bag is quite unproblematic. Cases can have additional accessory storage for things like the Apple Pencil or charger, which simplifies your traveling setup.
3. Style ranges from cases to sleeves, with various designs, colors, and materials to show your style. Whether it be sleek leather or fun and colorful, there's something for every taste.

In other words, an iPad sleeve or case protects in style: it keeps your device safe and your personality at its glorious best.

9. AirPods Pro (or Other Bluetooth Headphones)

Wireless audio accessories, such as the AirPods Pro, were made to enhance the listening experience when using the iPad 11.

1. High-Quality Sound: The AirPods Pro avails quality high-fidelity audio to make it perfect for movie time, music, or video calls. The quality is that of high-end headphones, and this allows you to enjoy good sound. It's like upgrading your iPad's built-in speakers to a personal concert experience.

2. Active Noise Cancellation: AirPods Pro introduces active noise cancellation to block ambient noises, thus allowing focused listening. This is quite useful if you happen to work in the middle of a noisy area; it lets you focus on your audio without diversion.

3. Seamless Integration: The AirPods Pro would connect seamlessly with the iPad via Bluetooth, have seamless device switching, and are easy to pair within the Apple ecosystem. The ease of just popping them in your ears and having them immediately connect is like having a wireless extension of your iPad.

In all, high-quality sound, convenience, noise isolation- all these features make AirPods Pro or any other Bluetooth headphones further justify why an iPad experience feels complete with these accessories.

10. Portable Power Bank

Portable power bank means a battery pack, providing some additional charging power while on the go to your iPad.

1. Extended Power: The main work of the portable power bank is for recharging your iPad when you are not close to a power outlet. This shall be useful during long trips, camping, or any situation where

electricity is not available. It acts just like a spare battery that keeps your gadget running.

2. Multiple Charges: Most of the power banks come in all capacities and hence are able to provide your iPad with multiple charges. In such a case, you can just keep on using your gadget without searching for an outlet. Just like carrying extra fuel in your car, a backup fuel tank for the iPad will keep it going at the most essential moment.

3. Flexible Charging: Many portable power banks have several ports, providing not only iPad charging but also other devices like smartphones or wireless headphones, all at the same time. This has made it a very important tool for anyone relying on more than one device in their activities.

In a nutshell, a portable power bank no doubt represents an essential gadget that will keep your iPad and other devices charged while you remain connected and productive throughout the day.

CHAPTER 2: UNLOCKING THE POWER OF YOUR NEW IPAD: A SEAMLESS SETUP GUIDE

GETTING STARTED WITH YOUR IPAD: THE ESSENTIAL SETUP PROCESS

Getting your iPad up and running is a breeze, whether you're a tech novice or a seasoned pro. Here's how to kick off your iPad journey effortlessly.

PREPPING FOR SMOOTH SAILING

Before diving into the setup process, gather these essentials for a hassle-free experience:

1) **Internet Connection:** Ensure you have access to a Wi-Fi network or cellular data service. Have the network name and password handy for Wi-Fi setup, especially if you're opting for Wi-Fi + Cellular models.

2) **Apple ID and Password:** If you already have an Apple ID, great! Make sure you have your credentials handy. If not, fret not! You can easily create one during the setup process.

3) **Payment Information:** Planning to utilize Apple Pay? Have your payment card account details ready to seamlessly add a card during setup.

4) **Previous Device or Backup:** If you're upgrading from a previous iPad or have a backup of your device, keep it nearby. You'll need it to smoothly transfer your data to your new iPad.

a) **Tip:** Running low on storage for a backup? iCloud has you covered. You can obtain additional storage space free of charge for up to three weeks from your iPad purchase. Simply head to **Settings > General > Transfer or Reset [device]** on your previous device, tap **Get Started**, and follow the prompts.

5) **Android Device:** Switching from an Android device? No worries! Keep your Android device handy for a seamless transfer of your Android content.

TURNING ON YOUR IPAD

1. To power on your iPad, simply Long-Press the top button till the iconic Apple logo graces your screen.

Troubleshooting Tip: Battery Woes?

a) In case your iPad doesn't spring to life, it might be running low on battery. Give it a boost by connecting it to a charger. For further assistance, refer to the Apple Support article "If your iPad won't turn on or is frozen."

Accessibility Made Easy

a) **For Visually Impaired Users:** If you're visually impaired, activating VoiceOver, the screen reader, is a breeze. On iPads with a Home button, triple-click it; for other models, triple-click the top button. Additionally, you can enable Zoom by double-tapping the screen with three fingers.

2) Choose any of the following methods:
   a) **Quick Start (for iOS 11, iPadOS 13, or newer:** If you possess a different iPhone or iPad with compatible software, make use of Quick Start. Simply bring your old and new devices close together, and follow the onscreen prompts to seamlessly transfer preferences, settings and iCloud Keychain securely. You can then complete the process by restoring the remaining data and content from your iCloud backup. Alternatively, if both devices are running iPadOS 13, iOS 12.4, or later, opt for wireless data transfer. Keep both devices nearby and connected to a power source until the data migration process is complete.
   b) **Manual Setup:** Prefer a hands-on approach? Tap "Set Up Manually."
3) Proceed by following the straightforward onscreen instructions to complete the setup process.

SWITCHING FROM ANDROID PHONE TO IPAD: SEAMLESSLY TRANSFER YOUR DATA

If you're making the leap from an Android device to an iPad, worry not! You can effortlessly transfer all your data using the Move to iOS application during the initial setup of your new iPad.

Note: If you've already completed the setup process and now wish to utilize Move to iOS, you have two options: either erase your iPad and start anew or transfer your data manually.

1) **Via your smartphone:**
   a) Ensure your device is running Android version 4.0 or later.
2) **On Your iPad:**

a) Adhere to the setup assistant as usual.
b) When prompted on the "Transfer Your Apps & Data" screen, tap "From Android."
3) **Via your smartphone:**
a) Turn on Wi-Fi.
b) Access the Move to iOS application.
c) Follow the straightforward onscreen instructions to initiate the data transfer process.

Warning: Prioritize your safety! Prior to exploring your iPad experience, ensure you're well-versed with the important safety information.

MASTERING IPAD'S POWER MANAGEMENT: WAKE, UNLOCK, AND LOCK WITH EASE

Your iPad is designed to conserve power and prioritize security by automatically turning off the display, locking itself, and entering sleep mode when not in use. Here's how you can swiftly wake, unlock, and lock your iPad to seamlessly resume your tasks.

WAKING YOUR IPAD

To awaken your iPad from its slumber, you have a couple of options:
1) **Press the Top Button:** Simply press the top button located on the device.
2) **Tap the Screen (supported models):** If your iPad supports this feature, a gentle tap on the screen will do the trick.

UNLOCKING IPAD WITH FACE ID

For iPad users fortunate enough to have Face ID, unlocking your device is a breeze:

1) **Tap the Screen:** Initiate the unlocking process by tapping the screen, then direct your gaze towards your iPad.
   a) Watch as the lock icon gracefully transitions from closed to open, indicating that your iPad is now unlocked.
2) **Swipe Up:** Complete the unlocking process by sliding upward from the base of the screen.

Locking Your iPad Again

To ensure the security of your iPad when not in use, simply hit the top button to lock it. Your iPad will also automatically lock if not interacted with for a minute or approximately a minute, conserving both power and security. However, if you've enabled Attention Aware Features in **Settings** > press **Face ID & Passcode**, your iPad won't reduce brightness or secure whenever it senses your attention, enhancing your uninterrupted experience.

EFFORTLESS UNLOCKING UTILIZING TOUCH ID

If you're the proud owner of an iPad utilizing a built-in fingerprint reader, unlocking your device is as simple as a touch. Here's steps to access your iPad utilizing Touch ID:

1) **On iPads with a Home Button:** Gently place your registered finger on Home button or the Power button.
2) **For iPads without a Home button (e.g. the iPad mini (7th gen):** Lightly press the top button with your finger with the embedded Touch ID sensor.

Once unlocked, to secure your iPad again, just tap the top button. If left idle, your iPad will self-lock after a brief time, ensuring both convenience and security.

UNLOCKING IPAD UTILIZING A PASSCODE

If you opted not to configure Touch ID or if you're using an iPad without Touch ID capabilities, fret not! Unlocking your iPad utilizing a Passcode is equally straightforward:
1) **Initiate Unlocking:**
   a) For iPads utilizing a Home button, simply tap the Home button.
   b) Regarding different iPad models, slide upward from the lower edge of the screen to go back to the Home screen.
2) **Enter Your Passcode:**
   a) Input your unique passcode to gain entry to your iPad's features and functionalities.

EFFORTLESS LOCKING OF YOUR IPAD

If you need to swiftly secure your iPad, just tap the top button. Your iPad will also automatically lock if left untouched for approximately a minute, ensuring both convenience and security.

INITIATE CELLULAR SERVICE ON YOUR IPAD (WI-FI AND CELLULAR VERSIONS)

For those with Wi-Fi and Cellular versions, accessing cellular data is a breeze, allowing you to keep in contact with the internet even when Wi-Fi isn't available.

To commence with cellular service, here's what you need to know:

1) **SIM Requirements:** Your cellular connection requires either an eSIM (on supported models) or a physical SIM. Please be aware that physical SIM cards are not supported with certain iPad Models.

2) **Connectivity Options:** Certain iPad models support connectivity to lightning-fast 5G networks.

STREAMLINE YOUR CONNECTIVITY: SETTING UP ESIM

Unlock the freedom of connectivity with eSIM for your iPad! Whether you travel often or just want a seamless experience cellular service, eSIM offers a seamless solution right at your fingertips.

Step-by-Step Activation:

1) Navigate to **Settings** > then press **Cellular Data**.

2) Choose your path:
   a) **Initializing your first cellular plan**: Select your preferred carrier and proceed with the guided setup instructions.

3) **Adding a New Plan**: Tap "Add a New Plan" to initiate the process.

4) **QR Code Activation**: Opting for a QR code? Tap "Other" and position your iPad to capture the QR code issued through your service provider. Alternatively, manually enter the details if needed. Be prepared to input any confirmation codes if prompted by your carrier.

Bonus: Carrier App Activation

a) Some carriers offer the convenience of activating your mobile plan via their dedicated app. Simply head to the App Store, install your carrier's application, and adhere to the instructions to purchase and activate your desired plan.

While you can store multiple eSIMs on your iPad, remember that only one can be used at a time. Switching between plans is a breeze—just navigate to **Settings** > then press **Cellular Data**, and select the desired plan from the list under "SIMs."

TRADITIONAL CONNECTIVITY: INSTALLING A PHYSICAL SIM

While eSIM offers a modern solution for connectivity, sometimes you need the reliability of a traditional SIM card. Here's how to seamlessly install a nano-SIM card on your iPad.

Step-by-Step Guide:

1) Locate the small hole on the SIM tray of your iPad.
   a) Use SIM eject tool or a paper clip to gently push into the hole, ejecting the tray from the iPad.

2) Carefully extract the tray from your iPad once it's ejected.

3) Place the nano-SIM card into the tray, making certain the angled corner matches the specified slot.

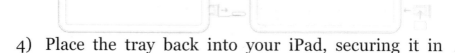

4) Place the tray back into your iPad, securing it in place.
5) If you've previously established a PIN for the SIM card, enter it when prompted.

Caution: Avoid guessing the PIN, as incorrect attempts may permanently disable your SIM card. Refer to Apple Support for guidance on managing SIM PINs.

Note: The design and position of the SIM tray may vary depending on the model of your iPad and region.

SEAMLESS MOBILE DATA CONTROL: MANAGE YOUR USAGE GAIN

The power to monitor your mobile data directly from your iPad. Whether you're conserving data, optimizing network preferences, or setting up a personal hotspot, it's all within your reach.

Step-by-Step Instructions:

1) Access **Settings** > then press **Cellular Data** on your iPad.
2) Explore the following options:
   a) To limit data usage to Wi-Fi only, toggle off Cellular Data.
   b) Customize your network preferences by toggling 5G, roaming, or LTE settings under Cellular Data Options.
   c) Enable Personal Hotspot functionality by tapping **Set Up Personal Hotspot** (availability

may vary by Service provider), then proceed as directed on the screen.

d) Administer your mobile service account effortlessly by tapping Manage [account name] or Carrier Services.

Crucial Information:

1) Note that when utilizing cellular services via GSM networks, a digital SIM or external SIM card is required. For CDMA networks, a third-party SIM is necessary.

2) Your iPad's cellular capabilities are subject to the policies of your telecommunications provider, which may entail restrictions on switching providers and roaming options, even post-contract termination. For comprehensive details, reach out to your mobile carrier.

3) The accessibility of mobile functionalities is contingent upon various factors including the cellular network, the model of your iPad, and your geographical location.

SEAMLESS CONNECTIVITY: GETTING YOUR IPAD ONLINE

Bringing your iPad online is a breeze with Wi-Fi or cellular networks. Follow these straightforward steps to connect to the internet effortlessly.

CONNECTING TO A WI-FI NETWORK:

1) Navigate to **Settings** > **Wi-Fi** on your iPad and toggle Wi-Fi to on.

2) Choose any of the following options:
   a) Select a network from the list provided and enter the password if prompted.
   b) Opt for "Other" to join a hidden network. Enter the network's name, security type, and password as required.

Once connected, a Wi-Fi symbol 📶 will appear at the top of your screen, indicating a successful connection. You can verify this by launching Safari and visiting a webpage. Your iPad will automatically reconnect to known networks when you're back in range.

HARNESSING MOBILE CONNECTIVITY: JOINING A PERSONAL HOTSPOT

Maximize your connectivity by tapping into a shared Personal Hotspot from your iPhone or another iPad equipped with cellular capabilities. Here's how you can seamlessly connect to the internet using your iPad through a Personal Hotspot:

Step-by-Step Guide:

1. Navigate to **Settings** ⚙ > press **Wi-Fi** on your iPad.
2. Select the device name that is providing the Personal Hotspot.
3. If your iPad asks for a password, input the one shown in **Settings** ⚙ > **Cellular** > **Personal Hotspot** on the device providing the hotspot.

CONNECTING TO A MOBILE NETWORK (WI-FI AND CELLULAR VERSIONS):

When Wi-Fi isn't available, your iPad automatically switches to your carrier's cellular data network. If you encounter any connectivity issues, follow these troubleshooting steps:

1. Ensure that your SIM card is activated and unlocked. Refer to "Set up cellular service on iPad (Wi-Fi + Cellular models)" for assistance.

2. Navigate to **Settings** > then press **Cellular Data**.

3. Confirm that **Cellular Data** is toggled on.

When you're in need of an internet connection, your iPad takes the following steps, prioritizing seamless connectivity until the connection is established:

1. **Attempts to Connect to the Last Used Wi-Fi Network:** Your iPad automatically tries to reconnect to the most recently used available Wi-Fi network, streamlining your access to familiar connections.

2. **Displays Available Wi-Fi Networks:** If the most recent network isn't available, your iPad presents a list of Wi-Fi networks within range. You can pick the network you prefer to connect to, ensuring personalized access to the internet.

3. **Connects to Your Carrier's Mobile Data Network (Wi-Fi + Cellular Models):** In the absence of a Wi-Fi connection, your iPad seamlessly transitions to utilizing your carrier's cellular data network, providing uninterrupted access to the online world.

5G Connectivity Consideration: For iPads supporting 5G technology, your device may prioritize using 5G cellular data over Wi-Fi. If utilizing 5G, you'll notice the label "Using 5G Cellular For Internet" beneath the Wi-Fi network's name. To revert to Wi-Fi, simply tap the icon ⓘ adjacent to the network name and select "Use Wi-Fi for Internet".

Important Notes: In instances where a Wi-Fi connection isn't available, certain applications and services may send data over your carrier's cellular network. Be mindful that this may incur additional fees, depending on your cellular data plan. For detailed information regarding your plan rates, reach out to your carrier.

UNLOCK THE POTENTIAL OF YOUR IPAD WITH APPLE ID AND ICLOUD

SEAMLESS ACCESS TO A WORLD OF SERVICES

Your Apple ID opens the door to a multitude of Apple services, granting you access to the wonders of the App Store, the iTunes Store, Apple Books, Apple Music, FaceTime, iCloud, iMessage, and beyond.

Signing in with Ease

If you missed signing in during the initial setup, fret not. Follow these simple steps to get started:

1) **Navigate to Settings**: Locate the **Settings** icon on your iPad's home screen.
2) **Tap Sign in to Your iPad**: Click on this option to kickstart the process.

3) **Choose Your Preferred Method**:
   a) Sign in with a nearby iPhone or iPad: Opt for this option and adhere to the instructions to sync with another Apple device.
   b) Sign in manually: Input your email address or phone number along with the associated password. If you don't possess an Apple ID yet, you can swiftly create one.
4) **Verify with Two-Factor Authentication**: For added security, input the six-digit verification code if you've enabled two-factor authentication.

Take Control of Your Apple ID: Customize Your Settings

Tailor Your Experience to Suit Your Needs

Managing your Apple ID preferences ensures that your digital world aligns perfectly with your preferences. Here's how to do it:

1) **Navigate to Settings**: Tap on the **Settings** icon and then select "[Your Name]".
2) **Customize Your Preferences**: Choose from a range of options:
   a) Update your contact information.
   b) Change your password for enhanced security.
   c) Manage Account Recovery Contacts for added peace of mind.
   d) Utilize iCloud for seamless data synchronization.
   e) Review and control your subscriptions effortlessly.
   f) Keep your payment methods and billing address up to date.
   g) Manage Family Sharing to maintain communication with your loved ones.

Effortless Storage and Synchronization Across Devices
iCloud serves as your digital vault, securely storing photographs, documents, videos, backups, and more, while seamlessly updating them across all your devices. This automatic synchronization ensures that your digital life remains effortlessly organized.

Key Benefits of iCloud:

1) Share photos, calendars, notes, folders, and files with ease.

2) Enjoy a g-mail account and 5 GB of complimentary storage for your files.

3) For those needing increased capacity and enhanced functionalities, iCloud+ offers a subscription service.

Note: Certain iCloud features may have specific system requirements. Additionally, the availability of iCloud and its features may vary by country or region.

Optimize Your iCloud Experience: Personalize Your Settings

Maximize the Complete Capabilities of iCloud for Seamless Integration

To tailor your iCloud experience to suit your needs, follow these simple steps after signing in with your Apple ID:

1) **Access iCloud Settings**: Head to **Settings > [Your Name] > iCloud**.

2) **Customize to Your Liking**:
   a) Check your iCloud storage status effortlessly.
   b) Activate the features that align with your preferences, such as Photos, iCloud Drive, and iCloud Backup.

Discover the Versatility of iCloud on Your iPad

Effortless Backups and Synchronization Across Devices
Make the most of iCloud's capabilities on your iPad with these invaluable features:

1) **Automated Backups**: Ensure your iPad stays backed up automatically, providing you with peace of mind.

Key Uses of iCloud on iPad:

a) **Photos and Videos**: Utilize iCloud Photos to store and access your visual memories effortlessly.

b) **Files and Documents**: Keep Everything in Order with iCloud Drive, ensuring your important files are accessible from any device.

c) **Email**: Access your iCloud Mail conveniently from your iPad.

d) **Contacts, Notes, Calendars, and Reminders**: Keep your essential info. Current throughout all your Apple gadgets.

e) **Third-Party App Data**: Enjoy seamless synchronization of data from supported external applications and games.

f) **Messages**: Set up Messages on your iPad to ensure your conversations are in sync across devices.

g) **Credentials and Transaction Methods:** Ensure your passkeys and payment methods are available across all your gadgets utilizing iPad and iCloud Keychain.

h) **Safari Bookmarks and Open Tabs**: Keep your browsing experience consistent by syncing Safari bookmarks and open tabs across your devices. Discover how to bookmark websites and manage tabs efficiently on your iPad.

i) **News, Stocks, and Weather Settings**: Customize your News, Stocks, and Weather preferences effortlessly, with changes reflected across all your gadgets.

j) **Home and Health Data**: Safeguard your home and health data by keeping it stored and up to date on iCloud, ensuring seamless access and synchronization across devices.

k) **Voice Memos**: Capture your thoughts and ideas on the go with Voice Memos, knowing they're securely stored and accessible across your Apple devices.

l) **Map Favorites**: Keep your favorite locations and routes readily available by syncing Map favorites across your devices, ensuring you're always prepared for your next journey.

Additionally, you have the power to:

m) **Share Photographs and Videos**: Establish communal albums in Photos on your iPad and join or set up an iCloud Shared Photo Library, ensuring seamless sharing of precious memories with loved ones.

n) **Collaborate with iCloud Drive**: Share directories and documents effortlessly using iCloud Drive on your iPad, simplifying collaboration and file management.

o) **Use Find My:** Track down a lost device or share your whereabouts with loved ones using the Find My feature.

For enhanced features such as Hide My Email, iCloud Private Relay, and HomeKit Secure Video support, consider subscribing to iCloud+ for additional storage and access.

Furthermore, your iCloud data isn't limited to your iPad; it's available for you to use across a range of devices including iPhone, Windows computer, MacBook, Apple TV, Apple Watch, and iCloud.com.

EFFORTLESSLY NAVIGATE YOUR IPAD SETTINGS

Discover and Customize Settings with Ease
Within the Settings app, you have the ability to tailor your iPad experience to your preferences. Here's how to find and modify settings:

1. **Access Settings**: Locate the **Settings** app on your Home Screen or in the App Library, then tap to open it.

2. **Search for Settings**: Swipe down on the sidebar to unveil the search field. Tap on the search field at the top left, and enter a term such as "volume." Once entered, tap on a setting listed on the left of the screen to access it directly.

Pro Tip: Simplify your search by accessing settings directly from the Home Screen or Lock Screen.

OPTIMIZE YOUR COMMUNICATION: CONFIGURE CONTACTS, MAIL, AND CALENDAR ACCOUNTS ON IPAD

Easily Connect with Your Favorite Services
Beyond the built-in apps and iCloud, your iPad also integrates smoothly with Microsoft Exchange and a plethora of widely-used online email, contact, and calendar services. Adhere to these instructions to create accounts for these services:

SETTING UP A MAIL ACCOUNT

1) **Access Settings**: Navigate to **Settings** >press **Mail** > then press **Accounts > Add Account**.
2) **Choose Your Service**:
   a) Select a service, such as iCloud or Microsoft Exchange, and input your account details.

b) Alternatively, tap "Other," then "Add Mail Account," and please input your login credentials.

SETTING UP A CONTACTS ACCOUNT

1) **Access Settings**: Navigate to **Settings** ⊚ > press **Contacts** > then press **Accounts** > **Add Account**.
2) **Choose Your Service**:
   a) Tap a service like iCloud or Microsoft Exchange, and provide your account details.
   b) Alternatively, tap "Other," then "Add LDAP Account" or "Add CardDAV Account" (if supported by your organization), and Input the server and account details.

SETTING UP A CALENDAR ACCOUNT

1) **Access Settings**: Navigate to **Settings** ⊚ > press **Calendar** > then press **Accounts** > and select **Add Account**.
2) **Select Your Preferred Method**:
   a) Opt for a service like iCloud or Microsoft Exchange, and input your account details.
   b) Alternatively, tap "Other," then "Add CalDAV Account," and provide the server and account detail.
   c) To add to iCal (.ics) calendars, press "Other," then "Add Subscribed Calendar," and input the URL of the .ics file or import it from Mail.

Additionally, by enabling iCloud Keychain on the iPad, then your accounts remain synchronized across all your gadgets where iCloud Keychain is activated.

UNLOCKING THE SECRETS OF IPAD STATUS ICONS

Deciphering the Symbols That Guide Your iPad Experience

Exploring the world of iPad status icons opens a door to understanding your device's operations at a glance. These symbols, nestled in the upper echelon of your screen, serve as silent messengers, relaying vital information about your iPad's connectivity and settings. Fear not, for navigating this symbolic landscape is simpler than you may imagine.

Decoding the Symbols: What They Reveal

1) **Wi-Fi Icon** 🛜 : This icon signifies your iPad's connection to the vast expanse of the internet via Wi-Fi. The more bars, the stronger the connection—a beacon of seamless connectivity awaits.

2) **Cell Signal** 📶 : For those wielding the power of Wi-Fi + Cellular models, this icon denotes proximity to the cellular network. Should you encounter a barren landscape devoid of signal, fret not; "No service" shall be your guide.

3) **Airplane Mode** ✈ : A versatile ally in the realm of travel, Airplane mode offers a sanctuary for non-wireless activities while potentially grounding wireless functions.

4) **5G** 5G : Witness the dawn of a new era with your carrier's 5G network, beckoning forth supported models to indulge in internet connectivity like never before.

5) **5G UC** 5G⁵꜀ : Behold, the carrier's 5G UC network, beckoning forth with the promise of higher frequency versions of 5G. Supported models stand poised to harness this power, delving into realms of internet connectivity previously unimagined.

6) **5G+** 5G+ : Step into the realm of 5G+ networks, where carriers unleash the full potential of higher frequency 5G variants. Supported models revel in the opportunity to traverse this expanse of connectivity, transcending boundaries and limitations.

7) **5G UW** 5G⁵ᵥᵥ : Witness the dawn of a new era with the carrier's 5G UW network, offering access to higher frequency iterations of 5G technology. Supported models embrace this opportunity to elevate their internet connectivity, forging paths to digital innovation.

8) **5G E** 5G E : Behold, the carrier's 5G E network, heralding the inception of advanced networking for supported models. Embrace the opportunity to experience enhanced internet speeds and performance, elevating your digital interactions to new heights.

9) **LTE** LTE : Delve into the realm of 4G LTE networks, the stalwart backbone of modern connectivity. Supported models seamlessly connect to this network, ensuring swift and reliable internet access wherever you roam.

10) **4G** 4G : Traverse the landscape of 4G networks, offering a robust foundation for internet connectivity on supported iPad models. Experience the

convenience of uninterrupted access to online resources, regardless of your geographic location.

11) **3G** 3G : Journey back to the origins of cellular connectivity with the enduring 3G network. Though surpassed by its successors in speed and performance, 3G remains a reliable option for connecting to the web on supported iPad models.

12) **EDGE** EDGE: Experience connectivity on the EDGE network, ensuring access to online resources on supported iPad models.

13) **GPRS** GPRS: Embrace the reliability of GPRS network connectivity, facilitating seamless internet access on supported iPad models.

14) **Personal Hotspot Connection** : Witness the power of sharing internet connectivity through the Personal Hotspot feature of another device. Seamlessly join a Personal Hotspot to expand your connectivity horizons.

15) **VPN** : Secure your connection and access private networks with ease using VPN technology on your iPad.

16) **Navigation** : Transform your iPad into a navigation companion with turn-by-turn directions, guiding you effortlessly to your destination.

17) **Personal Hotspot** : Transform your iPad into a source of internet connectivity for other devices with the Personal Hotspot feature.

18) **Phone Call** : Seamlessly place and answer phone calls directly on your iPad, expanding its functionality beyond mere internet browsing.

19) **FaceTime** : Engage in face-to-face communication with pals, relatives, and colleagues using the FaceTime feature on your iPad.

20) **Screen Recording** : Witness the power of capturing your iPad's screen in action, a feature facilitated by the screen recording icon.

21) **Camera Active** : Stay informed about apps accessing your iPad's camera, ensuring you know when your visual data is being used.

22) **Microphone in Use** : Stay informed when apps access your iPad's microphone, ensuring transparency and control over audio recording activities.

23) **Syncing** : Witness the harmonious exchange of data as your iPad syncs with your computer, ensuring seamless integration across devices.

24) **Network Activity** : Stay vigilant with the network activity icon, signaling ongoing communication or data exchange within your device's digital ecosystem.

25) **Lock** : Ensure the safety of your iPad with the lock icon, indicating when your device is securely locked.

26) **Do Not Disturb** : Embrace moments of uninterrupted focus with the Do Not Disturb icon, signaling when this feature is activated.

27) **Orientation Lock** : Maintain your preferred screen orientation with the orientation lock icon, ensuring stability in your viewing experience.

28) **Location Services** : Be aware of when apps access your iPad's location services, allowing you to control the dissemination of location information.

29) **Alarm** : Stay punctual with the alarm icon, indicating when an alarm is set within your device.

30) **Headphones Connected** : Experience the joy of seamless audio with the headphones connected icon, signaling successful pairing with Bluetooth® headphones.

31) **Battery** : Stay informed about your iPad's power status with the battery icon, displaying the battery level or charging status.

32) **Battery Charging** : Keep your iPad powered up and ready for action with the battery charging icon, indicating when your device is receiving power.

33) **Bluetooth Battery** : Monitor the battery level of paired Bluetooth devices with the Bluetooth battery icon, ensuring you stay connected without interruption.

34) **AirPlay** : Immerse yourself in a world of multimedia with the AirPlay icon, signaling when AirPlay is enabled for wireless streaming.

35) **Voice Control** : Utilize the capabilities of voice interaction with the Voice Control icon, indicating when this feature is enabled in **Settings** > **Accessibility**.

36) **RTT** : Embrace real-time text communication with the RTT icon, signaling when RTT is activated on your iPad.

CHARGING AND MONITORING YOUR IPAD BATTERY

Your iPad runs on an internal, lithium-ion rechargeable battery - the pinnacle of modern battery technology. With lithium-ion at its core, your device is equipped for optimal performance. Compared to traditional counterparts, lithium-ion batteries boast lighter weight, faster charging capabilities, extended lifespans, and heightened power density for prolonged usage.

Understanding the Charge

Monitoring your iPad's battery level is a breeze with the battery icon stationed at the upper-right corner of the status bar. Whether you're syncing data or actively using your device, the charging process may vary in duration. If your iPad's battery is running critically low, it may signal its need for a quick recharge by displaying an icon depicting a nearly drained battery. Patience is key in this scenario; allow for a maximum of 10 minutes of charging before resuming your activities. In cases of extreme depletion, your device may remain unresponsive for a maximum of 2 minutes before revealing the low-battery indicator.

Fueling Up: Charging Your iPad Battery

Charging Methods Made Easy Juicing up your iPad battery is a simple task with multiple options at your disposal. Choose from the following methods:

1) **Direct Power Outlet Connection:** Utilize the provided cord and power adaptor to establish a direct connection from your iPad to an electrical outlet. Refer to the "Power adapter and charge cable for iPad" for guidance.

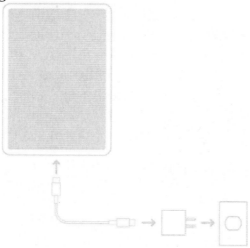

2) **Computer Connection:** Alternatively, link your iPad to your computer utilizing a compatible cable. Ensure that your computer is powered on during this process. Keep an eye out for the charging indicator on the battery icon to confirm that your iPad is replenishing its power reserves.

Powerful Insights When linking your iPad to a computer, be wary of potential power drainage if the computer is turned off. Confirm the charging status with the charging indicator ⚡. If your MacBook or PC lacks the necessary power output to power up your iPad effectively, a "Not Charging" message will be displayed within the status bar.

Important Note: While it may seem convenient, avoid attempting to power up your iPad through your keyboard unless it boasts a high-capacity USB port. Optimal charging requires a direct connection to a reliable power source.

Automated Backups and Syncing

Connecting your iPad to an electrical outlet isn't just about recharging; it can also trigger valuable processes like iCloud backup or syncing wirelessly with a computer.

Safety First

Exercise caution if you suspect any liquid presence in your iPad's charging port. Refrain from plugging the charging cord into it to prevent any potential damage.

Optimizing Battery Life

Remember, battery longevity and charging cycles are subject to variation based on usage and configurations. If you experience any issues or need support, please contact Apple or an authorized Apple service provider for help.

KEEPING TABS ON BATTERY LIFE

Instant Status Updates

Quickly check the remaining charge of your iPad battery right from the status bar. But why stop there? Enhance your monitoring capabilities by adding a widget to the Home Screen. This widget not only tracks your iPad battery but also keeps you informed about the battery status of connected accessories like AirPods and Apple Pencil.

Simple Setup

To display the iPad battery status in the status bar, navigate to **Settings** ⚙> then press **Battery**, then toggle on Battery Percentage. It's a simple procedure that provides instant access to crucial battery information.

UNLOCKING KNOWLEDGE: NAVIGATING AND BOOKMARKING THE IPAD MANUAL

Exploring Resources in Safari

Dive into the wealth of information offered by the iPad User Guide accessible through the Safari app. Discover how to tailor your experience, bookmark crucial sections, and even store it as a shortcut for effortless access from your Home Screen.

STEP-BY-STEP GUIDE

1) **Launch Safari:** Launch the Safari application on your iPad to embark on your journey of discovery.
2) **Access the Guide:** Navigate to https://support.apple.com/guide/ipad to immerse yourself in the iPad Manual.
3) **Customize Language and Region:** Tailor your experience by selecting your preferred language and country or region. Simply scroll to the bottom of the page, tap the country or region link (e.g., United States), and make your desired selection.

4) **Optimize Accessibility:** Ensure swift access to the guide by employing the following options:
   a) **Add to Home Screen:** Transform the guide into a convenient shortcut directly on your Home Screen, ready to assist you at a moment's notice.
   b) **Add Bookmark:** Seamlessly bookmark essential sections for easy retrieval. These bookmarks are accessible by tapping the bookmark icon in Safari and navigating to the Bookmarks section.

HARNESSING WISDOM: EXPLORING THE IPAD MANUAL LOCATED IN TIPS

Unlocking Insights in the Tips Application

Discover a treasure trove of knowledge within the Tips app, where the iPad Manual awaits your exploration.

Step-by-Step Guide

1) **Launch the Tips App:** Launch the Tips application on your iPad, signaling the beginning of your journey towards enriched understanding.
2) **Navigate to the iPad Manual:**
   a) **Scroll or Swipe:** Engage with the app interface by scrolling or swiping until you encounter the Tips collections.
   b) **Select iPad:** Within the collections, locate the iPad section nestled below User Guides, and tap to delve into the wealth of insights awaiting you.

CHAPTER 3: BASICS

UNLOCKING SOUND MASTERY: EFFORTLESSLY ADJUSTING VOLUME ON IPADOS 18

Discover the Simplicity of Managing Sound
Mastering the art of controlling volume on your iPad is simpler than you might think. Whether you're a tech novice, a seasoned user, or somewhere in between, navigating the volume settings is a breeze. Here's how:

UTILIZE THE VOLUME BUTTONS OR ENLIST SIRI'S ASSISTANCE

Tap into the potential of your device's physical volume buttons or engage Siri to tailor your sound experience precisely to your liking.

Volume Buttons: A Convenient Control at Your Fingertips
Located either on the side or upper part of your iPad, the volume buttons provide tactile control over media playback, notifications, and auditory cues. With a simple press, modify the volume of songs, videos, and more with ease.

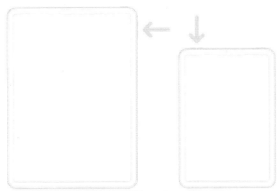

Siri: Your Personal Audio Assistant

Tap into the hands-free convenience of Siri to adjust volume effortlessly. Simply command Siri with phrases like "Turn up the volume" or "Turn down the volume," and watch as your iPad responds promptly to your vocal cues.

Harness Control Center for Instant Silencing

Take advantage of Control Center to swiftly mute sound warnings and notifications, ensuring uninterrupted focus when needed.

Important Safety Note: Protecting Your Hearing

As you explore the world of sound on your iPad, remember to prioritize your hearing health.

Please Note: Do Not Disturb and Audio Playback

Keep in mind that while Do Not Disturb mode enhances tranquility by muting notifications, it does not affect audio playback from podcasts, music, movies, or TV shows.

LOCKING RINGER AND NOTIFICATION VOLUMES

Navigate to **Settings** 🔘 > press **Sounds** and disable "Change with Buttons" to maintain consistent Ringer and Notification Volumes, regardless of button adjustments.

STREAMLINING VOLUME CONTROL WITH CONTROL CENTER

Whether your iPad is secured or you're engrossed in an app, Control Center offers a convenient avenue for volume adjustments. Simply swipe downwards from the top right to access Control Center, then adjust the volume 🔊 to your preference.

SAFEGUARDING HEARING WITH REDUCED HEADPHONE SOUNDS

Prioritize your auditory health by implementing precautions for headphone usage:

1. Navigate to **Settings** 🔘 > press **Sounds** > and then press **Headphone Safety**.
2. Activate "Reduce Loud Sounds" and fine-tune the maximum volume using the slider.

Family-Friendly Sound Settings

If you've configured Screen Time for a relative, you can ensure consistent sound safety by:

a) Enabling Content & Privacy Restrictions in **Settings** > press **Screen Time** > select then press **Content & Privacy Restrictions**.
b) Accessing "Reduce Loud Sounds" and selecting "Don't Allow" to prevent alterations to sound levels.

MUTING SOUND

Choose any of the following methods:

a) Long-Press the Volume Down button for instant muting.

b) Access Control Center by swiping down from the screen's top right, then tap the sound icon 🔔 to activate Silent mode. Repeat the action to restore sound.

TEMPORARY SILENCE FOR RING-INS, ALERT SIGNALS, AND NOTIFICATION MESSAGES

For a brief respite from incoming Ring-ins, Alert Signals, and Notification Messages:

a) Access Control Center by swiping down from the screen's top right, press "Focus," then select "Do Not Disturb."

MASTERING TOUCH: ESSENTIAL GESTURES FOR SEAMLESS IPAD INTERACTION

Unlock the Power of Intuitive Gestures
Embark on your journey to mastering iPad interaction by familiarizing yourself with a handful of fundamental gestures. From tapping to swiping, these actions empower you to navigate iPad and its apps effortlessly.

DISCOVER THE MAGIC OF GESTURES

Explore the following gestures and their corresponding actions:

1) **Tap** ● : Simply touch an item on the screen briefly with one finger. For instance, to launch an app, tap its icon on the Home Screen.

2) **Touch and Hold** ◎ : Press down on an item on the screen till a response occurs. For example, by touching and holding the wallpaper on the Home Screen, you initiate the app icons' jiggle mode.

3) **Swipe** ↑ : Glide one finger swiftly across the screen. For instance, swipe left on your Home Screen to reveal additional apps.

4) **Scroll** ↕ : Effortlessly Swipe one finger continuously across the screen to navigate through content. In apps like Photos, move a list upward or downward to reveal more items. Swipe for rapid scrolling, and display the screen to halt the movement.

5) **Zoom** ↗ : Harness the magic of zooming by placing 2 fingers on the display in close proximity. Spread them apart to zoom in and bring details closer, or draw them together to zoom out and gain a broader perspective.

Master Additional Zoom Techniques
Expand your zooming repertoire with these additional techniques:

6) Tap twice on a photo or webpage to instantly zoom in, then double-tap again to revisit to the original view.

7) In Maps, execute a double-tap and hold maneuver, then drag upwards to magnify or downwards to zoom

out, granting you precise control over your map exploration.

MASTERING ADVANCED IPAD GESTURES: UNLEASH THE FULL POTENTIAL

Unlock the complete capabilities of your iPad with advanced gesture controls. Whether you're new to it or have experience, mastering these gestures will streamline your interactions and enhance your productivity. Below, you'll find an in-depth manual for essential gestures, tailored for all iPad models.

Navigate Seamlessly: Discover Essential Gestures

1) **Go Home**: Simply slide upwards from the lower edge of your screen to revisit to the Home Screen effortlessly. This intuitive gesture ensures quick access to your preferred applications features, enhancing your overall iPad experience. (For iPads utilizing a Home button, the process may vary slightly.)

2) **Access Controls Instantly**: Need to adjust settings on the fly? Pull down from the upper-right edge to unveil Control Center swiftly. Here, you can conveniently toggle various controls and access additional options by long-pressing a control. Personalize your Control Center further by navigating to **Settings** > then press **Control**

Center, tailoring it to your preferences for seamless interaction.

3)   **Efficiently Launch the Application Switcher**: Streamline your ability to multitask by effortlessly opening the App Switcher. Simply slide upwards from the lower edge of your screen, pause briefly in the center, then lift your finger. This intuitive gesture grants you access to all open apps, enabling you to effortlessly navigate between them with ease. Explore your options by swiping right, then pick the application you want to dive back into your tasks. (For iPads utilizing a Home button, slight variations in the process may apply)

4)   **Seamlessly Switch Between Apps**: Enhance your productivity by swiftly switching between open apps with a simple gesture. Slide horizontally along the bottom boundary of your screen to seamlessly transition between your active applications. (On iPads utilizing a Home button, a subtle arc swipe facilitates the process.) This fluid movement empowers you to effortlessly juggle multiple tasks, ensuring a smooth and uninterrupted workflow.

5)   **Access the Dock within Apps**: Enhance your workflow within any application by swiftly accessing the Dock. Slide upwards from the lower

edge of your screen and pause momentarily to display the Dock, providing quick access to your favorite and frequently used apps. Pick the application you want within the Dock to seamlessly switch between tasks, optimizing your efficiency and productivity.

6) **Activate Siri with Ease**: Seamlessly interact with your iPad using Siri, your virtual assistant. Just say 'Siri' or 'Hey Siri,' long-press the top button to make a request. (For iPads utilizing a Home button, long-press the Home button instead.) Let go of the button after your request to quickly activate Siri's help.

7) **Accessibility Shortcut for Quick Access**: Enhance accessibility features utilizing a simple shortcut. Hit the top button thrice (or the Home button for iPads with a Home button) to swiftly open accessibility features. This convenient shortcut empowers users to customize their iPad experience, ensuring accessibility is readily available whenever needed.

8) **Capture Moments with Screenshot**: Preserve important moments and information with ease by taking screenshots on your iPad. Simply tap the top button briefly along with either volume button at the same time. (For iPads utilizing a Home

button, use the top button and the Home button.) This straightforward gesture captures your screen instantly, allowing you to save and share valuable content effortlessly. Perfect the skill of screenshotting and enhance your productivity on the go.

9)   **Power Off Your Device**: Ensure a smooth shutdown process with these straightforward steps. Simultaneously Long-hit the upper button in conjunction with any of the volume buttons till the sliders display on your screen. Then, effortlessly slide the top slider to switch off your iPad. (For iPads utilizing a Home button, simply Long-Hit the top button till the sliders display.) Alternatively, navigate to **Settings** > press **General** > then press **Shut Down** for an alternative method. Streamline your power-off process and ensure efficient management of your device's battery life.

10)   **Force Restart for Troubleshooting**: Resolve potential issues swiftly with a force restart. Tap the topmost volume button briefly, followed by the opposite volume button. Next, Long-Hit the top button till the iconic Apple logo displays on your screen. This action effectively restarts your device, providing a quick solution to any performance hiccups you may encounter. (For iPad mini 2021, note that the volume buttons are situated at the upper left.) Perfect the skill of force restarting and keep your iPad running smoothly at all times.

For users employing Magic Mouse or Magic Trackpad, explore additional functionalities with trackpad gestures or mouse actions tailored for your device. Enhance your iPad experience further by leveraging these advanced features and gestures seamlessly.

DISCOVERING THE MAGIC OF YOUR APPS: NAVIGATING IPAD'S INTERFACE

Unlocking the capabilities of your iPad begins with becoming proficient in navigating through your apps effortlessly. Here's an in-depth manual for help you seamlessly access and organize your apps on iPadOS 18.

OPENING APPS WITH EASE

1. **Access the Home Screen:** Start by sliding upward from the lower edge of your screen to access the Home Screen effortlessly. This simple gesture instantly takes you to the heart of your iPad's functionality.

2. **Explore Across Home Screen Pages**: Swipe left or right to explore the various Home Screen pages housing your apps. Effortlessly browse through your collection and discover the wealth of possibilities at your fingertips.

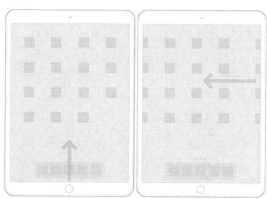

3. **Launching Apps**: When you locate the application you need, hit its icon on the Home Screen to open it instantly. With just a tap, dive into a world of productivity, entertainment, and creativity tailored to your preferences.

4. **Navigate Back with Ease**: To revisit to the first Home Screen page, simply slide upwards from the lower edge of the screen. This intuitive gesture ensures seamless navigation and keeps your iPad experience fluid and effortless.

EXPLORING THE APP LIBRARY

Delve deeper into your app collection with the innovative App Library feature, designed to streamline app organization and accessibility.

1) **Intelligent Categorization**: App Library intelligently groups your applications into categories like Productivity & Finance, Creativity, and Information & Reading. Your most frequently used apps are conveniently placed near the uppermost part of the screen and at the top level of their respective categories.

2) **Effortless Access**: Easily locate and open your favorite applications within the Application Library,

ensuring swift access to the tools and resources you need to enhance your iPad experience.

3) **Customization Options**: While apps in the Application Library are intelligently categorized, you have the flexibility to include them to the Home Screen for quick access. But, bear in mind that apps cannot be moved to different categories within the Application Library.

Navigating to App Library

1) **Accessing App Library from Home Screen**: Begin by navigating to the Home Screen, then slide left beyond all the Home Screen pages to reach the App Library. This seamless transition allows you to explore your app collection effortlessly.

2) **Quick Access from the Dock**: Alternatively, you can access the App Library swiftly by tapping the rightmost button in the Dock located at the lower part of your screen. This convenient shortcut provides instant access to your app repository, ensuring seamless navigation.

Finding Your App

2) **Search or Browse**: Upon entering the Application Library, press the search bar at the uppermost part of

the screen to enter the application name you're seeking. Alternatively, scroll through the list arranged alphabetically to browse through your apps.

3) **Opening the App**: Once you've located the desired app, simply tap on it to access it instantly. With just a tap, immerse yourself in the functionality and features of your chosen application.

4) **Exploring Categories**: If a category in the Application Library displays a few small application icons, tapping on them expands the category, revealing all the apps within it. This feature enhances organization and accessibility, allowing you to explore your apps efficiently.

Streamlining Your Home Screen: Simplifying App Access

Maximize the efficiency of utilizing your iPad by optimizing your Home Screen setup. With the innovative feature to toggle the visibility of Home Screen pages, you can tailor your device to suit your needs effortlessly.

Customizing The Pages on Your Home Screen

1. **Switch to Editing Mode:** Start by touching and holding the Home Screen until the apps enter editing mode, indicating that you've entered editing mode. This step grants you the freedom to customize your Home Screen layout according to your preferences.

2. **Access Page Thumbnails**: Tap the dots located near the screen's bottom to reveal miniature previews of your Home Screen pages. Each page is indicated by a thumbnail image, allowing you to visualize your layout easily.

3. **Hide or Show Pages**: To conceal certain pages, tap on the thumbnails to deselect the checkmarks below

them. Conversely, to reveal concealed pages, press on the thumbnails to select the checkmarks back.

4. **Finalize Your Changes**: Once you've adjusted the pages on your Home Screen to your liking, tap "Done" to confirm your changes. Your Home Screen layout is now customized to improve your browsing journey.

Enjoy Enhanced Navigation

With fewer pages on your Home Screen, you can seamlessly transition between your initial Home Screen page and the App Library with just a couple of strokes. This streamlined process brings the Application Library nearer to your primary workspace, ensuring quick access to all your apps whenever you need them.

Note: Keep in mind that when Home Screen pages are concealed, new applications downloaded from the Application Store may automatically be included to the Application Library in lieu of the Home Screen. This feature optimizes organization and ensures a clutter-free Home Screen experience.

Reordering Home Screen Pages

If your iPad's Home Screen is cluttered with multiple pages, fear not! You have the ability to rearrange them effortlessly. Imagine having all your favorite apps neatly arranged on your initial Home Screen page. Here's how:

1. **Initiate the Jiggle**: Long-press the Home Screen wallpaper until your applications start to jiggle, signaling that you're ready to rearrange.

2. **Navigate to the Pages**: Near the screen's bottom, you'll see dots indicating the pages on your Home

Screen. Tap on them to reveal thumbnail images of each page, with tick marks beneath them.

3. **Move with Precision**: To reorder, simply touch and hold the page you wish to relocate, then smoothly reposition it by dragging.

4. **Confirm Your Layout**: Once satisfied with the arrangement, tap "Done" to solidify your new Home Screen setup.

Changing Download Destinations

When you acquire new applications from the Application Store, you hold the reins on where they land – be it the Home Screen, App Library, or both. Take control of your app organization:

1. **Access Settings**: Head over to "Settings⊚" and then select "Home Screen & App Library."

2. **Decide Your Destination**: Here, you can opt to include new applications to both your Home Screen and Application Library or solely to the Application Library. The power to shape your digital space is in your hands.

Pro Tip: Want to keep track of notifications for apps stored in the Application Library? Simply toggle on "Show in App Library" to activate application notification badges.

Moving Apps with Ease

Have you ever transferred an app from your Home Screen to the Application Library and later had a change of heart? Fear not, as reversing the process is a breeze:

1. **Retrieve Your App**: Find the application you want to relocate from the Application Library.

2. **Initiate the Move**: Long-press on the app icon, then select "Add to Home Screen" (this option only appears if the app isn't already on your Home Screen).

EFFORTLESSLY NAVIGATE BETWEEN APPS ON YOUR IPAD

Seamless App Switching at Your Fingertips

Utilizing the Dock

Switching between apps on your iPad has never been smoother. With the Dock, you have instant access to your favorite and recently used applications, enabling you to effortlessly transition from one task to another:

1. **Access the Dock**: While in any app, simply slide upwards from the lower edge of the display to reveal the Dock. No need to swipe too far, just enough to bring it into view.

2. **Choose Your Destination**: Your favorite apps await you on the left of the Dock, while suggested apps, including recently used ones from your iPhone or Mac, are conveniently located on the right side.

3. **Navigate with Ease**: Once the Dock is visible, press on the application you like to switch to, and voilà! You're instantly transported to your desired destination.

Accessing the App Switcher

When it comes to managing your active apps, Split View setups, and Slide Over panels on your iPad, the Application Switcher is your go-to tool. Here's how to summon it effortlessly:

1. **Applicable to All iPad Models:** Slide upwards from the lower on the screen, then hold momentarily in the center. Alternatively, on iPads utilizing a Home button, simply click twice the Home button.

Pro Tip: No matter your iPad model, these methods grant you swift access to your active applications.

Browsing and Selecting Apps

Once within the Application Switcher, you'll find a panoramic view of all your active apps, Split View setups, and Slide Over panels. Here's how to navigate this digital landscape:

1. **Explore Open Applications**: Slide right to peruse your array of open applications. Pick the application you want or Split View workspace to seamlessly transition into it.

2. **Manage Slide Over Windows**: Swipe left to reveal your Slide Over windows. Easily switch between them by touching the window you wish to bring to the forefront.

Switching Between Open Apps

Now that you've acquainted yourself with the layout of the App Switcher, it's time to master app switching:

1. **Gesture Navigation**: Slide left or right with a single finger along the lower edge of the screen to effortlessly toggle between your open applications. (For iPads utilizing a Home button, execute this gesture in a slight arc

2. **Multi-Finger Maneuver**: Alternatively, employ a slide left or right utilizing four or five fingers for swift application switching.

ZOOMING AN APPLICATION TO OCCUPY THE ENTIRE SCREEN

While most iPhone apps are compatible with iPad, some may not utilize the complete capabilities the larger screen. Fear not, as you can easily zoom in on these apps to enhance your immersive experience:

1. **Zoom In**: If you find that an app isn't taking advantage of the iPad's expansive display, simply tap

   the zoom button to enlarge it. Tap the same

   button to revert to the original size.

Pro Tip: *Check the Application Store for an iPad-optimized version or a universal version designed for both iPhone and iPad to maximize your app's performance.*

QUITTING AND REOPENING APPS

Encountering an unresponsive app can be frustrating, but fear not, as troubleshooting is readily accessible:

1. **Quit the Application**: Access the Application Switcher by sliding upward from the lower edge of the display and then slide upward on the troublesome app to quit it.
2. **Reopen with Ease**: Return to the Home Screen or the Application Library and tap on the application to reopen it.

Pro Tip: If the issue persists, consider restarting your iPad for a fresh start.

MASTERING DRAG AND DROP: EFFORTLESSLY MOVE AND COPY ITEMS ON YOUR IPAD

Unlock the Power of Drag and Drop
With the intuitive drag and drop feature on your iPad, then the possibilities are endless. Whether you're a novice or a seasoned professional, mastering this function can significantly enhance your productivity. Imagine seamlessly moving text or items within an app or effortlessly copying content from one app to another. The convenience is unparalleled, and the learning curve is surprisingly gentle.

MOVING ITEMS WITH EASE

1. First, simply touch and hold the item you wish to relocate. If it's text, ensure you've selected it beforehand.
2. While keeping your finger pressed down, effortlessly drag the item to your desired location within the app.

Pro tip: When dragging an item within a lengthy document, rest assured that the screen will instinctively scroll to accommodate your movement, ensuring a smooth experience every time.

COPYING ACROSS APPS MADE SIMPLE

1) To duplicate an item between two open apps, initiate Split View or Slide Over.
2) Once you've arranged your apps accordingly, touch and hold-down the item you intend to copy until it hovers. Remember to select the text if necessary.
3) **Drag to Another App**

   a) As you drag an item, a visual indicator guides you to the exact spot where you can deposit it.
   b) When dealing with lengthy documents, rest assured that the document will smoothly scroll as you drag towards the top or bottom.

Pro Tip: For even smoother transfers, ensure the destination app is open before initiating the drag action. This way, you can directly drop the item into the recent message or email.

DRAG A LINK TO A SPLIT VIEW OR SLIDE OVER PANE

When dealing with links, you have even more flexibility:

1) Long-Press the link until it hovers.
2) Now, depending on your preference:
   a) To substitute a Split View or Slide Over window utilizing the link's destination, simply move the link to the window.
   b) Alternatively, if there's no Split View or Slide Over window visible:
      i) Swipe the link to either side of the screen to access the destination in Split View.
      ii) Alternatively, move the link near the edge to access it in Slide Over.

EFFORTLESS ITEM COPYING: SEAMLESSLY TRANSFER TO APPS ON YOUR HOME SCREEN OR DOCK

Expanding your productivity horizons is as easy as copying items to apps on your iPad's home screen or dock. By following these simple steps, you'll quickly master navigating your digital workspace:

1) **Touch and Hold to Copy**
   a) Start by gently pressing and holding the item you want to duplicate. For text, make sure it is highlighted first.
2) **Access the Dock or Home Screen**
   a) While still holding the item, employ another finger to slide upwards from the lower edge of the screen. Pause momentarily to reveal the Dock.
   b) Alternatively, press the Home button on iPads equipped with one.
3) **Drag and Drop**
   a) Now, with the item still held, drag it over the desired app icon on the Dock or home screen. As

you drag, an ethereal reflection of the item accompanies your finger.

Pro Tip: Navigate within the app by dragging over items to precisely choose the drop location. A visual indicator ⊕ guides you to the appropriate spot.

For instance, you can glide over the list of notes to pinpoint the exact note where you intend to place the item. Alternatively, utilize another finger to open a new note for dropping.

Should you have a change of heart mid-action, just release your finger before moving or drag the item out of view to cancel the process.

EFFORTLESS BULK SELECTION: STREAMLINING YOUR MOVE OPERATIONS

Maximize your efficiency by selecting and moving multiple items simultaneously on your iPad. With these simple steps, you'll be breezing through your tasks in no time:

1) **Touch, Hold, and Drag**
   a) Begin by touching and holding the first item you wish to select.
   b) Now, drag it slightly while continuing to grip it firmly.

2) **Tap to Add**
   a) While still holding the first item, employ another finger to tap on additional items you like to include in the selection.
   b) Keep an eye out for the badge that indicates the total number of items you've selected.

3) **Drag with Ease**
   a) With all desired items selected, seamlessly drag them together to their new destination.

Pro Tip: Should you have a change of heart mid-action, just release your finger before moving or drag the item out of view to cancel the process.

MASTERING MULTITASKING: HARNESSING THE POWER OF MULTIPLE APPLICATIONS ON YOUR IPAD

UNLOCKING SIMULTANEOUS PRODUCTIVITY

On your iPad, juggling multiple tasks has never been easier. With the Split View feature, you can seamlessly work across two dissimilar applications or windows from identical application, all within resizable views. Let's dive into how you can effortlessly open and manage multiple applications at once:

Display Two Items Side by Side

Picture this: You're texting a friend while checking directions on Maps, all without switching between apps. Here's how you can achieve this level of multitasking prowess:

1) **Initiate Split View**
   a) While utilizing an application, locate the 3 dots

   ••• at the uppermost part of the screen and tap on them.

   b) Next, tap on the Split View icon ⬓ (either ◧

   or ◧, depending on your preference) to position the recent application on either the right or left side of the screen.
2) **Select Your Second App**

a) Once the current application repositions to the side, revealing the Home Screen and Dock, navigate to the second application you like to open.
b) Pick the application you want icon either on your Home Screen or within the Dock.

Voila! You now have two apps seamlessly displayed adjacent in Split View, ready for simultaneous action.

Enhancing Efficiency: Seamlessly Swap Apps in Split View

Optimizing Your Workspace

In the world of multitasking on your iPad, flexibility is key. With Split View, not only can you work across two apps simultaneously, however you can also easily replace one app with another. Here's how you can effortlessly swap apps to suit your evolving needs:

Substitute an Application in Split View

Imagine you're midway through a project, and you realize you need to switch one of the apps you're working with. No problem! Adhere to these instructions to seamlessly Substitute an Application in Split View:

1) **Swipe Down to Reveal Options**

a) From the uppermost part of the application wish to substitute, slide downward from the 3 dots••• located at the uppermost part of the screen.

b) As you do this, the application you like to substitute gracefully drops down, making space for the new app.

2) **Select Your Replacement App**

a) With the original app now in a lowered position, navigate to the alternative application on your Home Screen or within the Dock.

b) Pick the application you want icon to initiate the swap.

In an instant, your workspace transforms as the two apps seamlessly switch places, now adjacent in Split View.

Pro Tip: Need more screen real estate for your multitasking endeavors? On supported models, head to **Settings** > then press **Display & Brightness**, press **Display Zoom**, and select **More Space**. This option increases pixel density, allowing you to view more content within your apps, especially handy when working across several windows in Split View.

Transforming Split View into Slide Over

Flexibility at Your Fingertips

In the dynamic world of multitasking on your iPad, versatility is key. Not only can you effortlessly work across two apps simultaneously in Split View, however you can also seamlessly transition any of them into a Slide Over window—a convenient smaller window that slides ahead of the primary app. Let's explore how you can effortlessly make this transition:

Transition from Split View to Slide Over

Picture this scenario: You're deep into a project, but suddenly you require immediate access to a different application without exiting the workspace you're currently using. No problem! Follow these simple steps to transform Split View into a Slide Over panel:

1) **Tap and Convert**

   a) Navigate to the upper section of the window you wish to convert into a Slide Over window.

   b) Tap on the icon ⠇ represented by three buttons.

   c) Next, select the rightmost button ▭, indicating the transition to Slide Over.

With just a couple of taps, your Split View setup transforms into a compact, yet easily accessible Slide Over window.

Pro Tip: Curious about opening an application in Slide Over? Refer to "Open an app in Slide Over" for further guidance. Additionally, on supported models, enjoy the added benefit of using Split View and Slide Over concurrently, maximizing your multitasking potential.

Switching back to Full Screen View.

Effortlessly Expand Your View

In the realm of juggling tasks on your iPad, adaptability is key. Utilizing Split View, you can seamlessly work across two apps simultaneously, but what if you need to return to a single full-screen view? Fear not! Here's how you can effortlessly maximize your workspace:

Revert to Full Screen View

Imagine you're wrapping up a project and ready to focus on a single app without distractions. Follow these straightforward steps to transition from Split View back to full-screen mode:

1) **Drag or Tap to Expand**
    a) One option is to simply Move the middle partition towards the screen's left or right boundary. This action automatically collapses one app, allowing the other to expand to full screen.

    b) Alternatively, tap on the icon••• located at the upper section of the application you wish to display in full screen mode, followed by, select the appropriate option from the menu that appears.

    c) Another method involves touching and holding the icon••• at the upper section of the application you like to display in full screen. While maintaining its upper edge uppermost part of the display, move it toward the center until its name and symbol appear. Once visible, release your finger to complete the action.

SWITCHING AN APPLICATION WINDOW TO A SLIDE OVER PANEL ON IPAD

Effortlessly Juggle Tasks with Slide Over

While you're engrossed in an app, you can seamlessly transition it into a Slide Over panel—a compact overlay that smoothly glides in front of another app or window—enabling you to open and operate a secondary app in the background. For instance, envision browsing through your Photos app while simultaneously engaging in a conversation on Messages, all within the convenience of your iPad.

Don't worry, your iPad efficiently handles the applications in Slide Over, allowing you to switch between them quickly and easily, enhancing your multitasking experience.

Access an Application in Slide Over

1) While immersed in an application, press the icon ●●● at the upper section of the screen, then select the desired app.
   a) Your current app gracefully shifts aside, revealing your Home Screen and Dock, ready to accommodate your multitasking journey.
2) Locate and launch the app you wish to have situated behind the Slide Over window.
3) Instantly, the second app springs to life, with the initial app gracefully positioned in a Slide Over window atop it.
4) For those equipped with supported models, should you desire to introduce a third app into Slide Over while your screen is in Split View, simply slide upwards from the lower edge to unveil the Dock. Then, effortlessly drag the third application from the Dock to the Split View divider.

Effortless App Navigation within Slide Over

To seamlessly glide between apps residing in Slide Over, embrace these intuitive gestures:

1) Glide your finger to the right across the base of the Slide Over panel. Alternatively:

   a) Begin the sliding gesture from the middle of the screen's height, starting at the lower edge of the Slide Over window.

   b) Pause briefly.

   c) Lift your finger, unveiling every Slide Over panels at your disposal.

2) If the app you seek is visible within the Slide Over window, simply tap on it to move it inside focus. Should it elude your immediate view, fear not. Engage in a fluid left and right swipe motion to seamlessly navigate through the lineup of apps at your disposal.

Utilizing the App Switcher

Feel empowered to leverage the App Switcher for effortless app navigation within Slide Over.

Customizing Slide Over Window Placement

Adapt the Slide Over panel to your preferred setup with these intuitive adjustments:

1) To relocate the Slide Over panel to the opposite edge of the display, effortlessly drag from the icon ••• at the upper section of the window.

2) Temporarily conceal the Slide Over panel by executing a full swipe upward from its bottom edge, or alternatively, swipe left •••. Alternatively, pull any part of the window's border towards the screen's left boundary. Witness as the Slide Over panel gracefully retreats, leaving behind a convenient tab as a reminder of its availability.

3) Retrieve the Slide Over panel from its temporary concealment by dragging the tab, indicative of the window's presence, from the left edge of the screen back onto the display area.

Switching from Slide Over to Split View

1) Initiate the transition by touching the icon^{•••} positioned at the upper section of the Slide Over panel.

2) Subsequently, tap on the icon [image], followed by selecting [image] either to allocate the current app to the screen's left boundary, or [image] to position it on the right.

3) For users with supported models, revel in the flexibility of concurrently utilizing Slide Over and Split View, enhancing your multitasking capabilities.

Centering Elements displayed on the Screen

Within various iPad apps, including Mail, Messages, Notes, and Files, you can effortlessly center items, ensuring convenient access to pivotal content.

1) Employ any one of these methods based on your app of choice:
   a) Long-press a message within an inbox in the Mail application.
   b) Extend the same gesture to conversations within Messages.
   c) Apply a touch-and-hold action to notes within the Notes app.

2) Simply tap on "Open in New Window" to summon the desired item into the center of your screen, overlaying your current view without altering your perspective.

3) **Pro Tip**: Engage in a pinch gesture to swiftly open any item outlined in the initial step directly within a

fresh pane at the center of your screen, offering unparalleled convenience and efficiency.

Customizing Window Display

Effortlessly tailor the display of your windows to align with your preferences:

1) Tap ▣ to expand the center window to full-screen mode.

2) Enhance productivity by transforming it into a Split View window with a tap on ⊓ .

3) Alternatively, convert it into a Slide Over panel by hitting ▭ .

EXPLORING APP WORKSPACES

Delve into the realm of app workspaces to unleash the complete capabilities your iPad's multitasking capabilities. In numerous apps such as Notes, Mail, Safari, and Files, you can seamlessly manage multiple open windows, including those within Split View and Slide Over.

Viewing an App's Open Windows

1) Employ any one of these methods to access an app's open windows:
   a) Execute a slide upwards from the lower edge of the screen to unveil the Dock.
   b) Navigate to the Home Screen, delivering an all-encompassing overview of all active windows within the selected app.

2) Long-press the application icon of your choice to reveal a host of options, then tap "Show All Windows."

a) Note: To avoid triggering the app jiggle mode inadvertently, ensure you don't hold the application icon for an extended period. If all apps start jiggling, tap "Done" or hit the Home button (on iPads utilizing a Home button) before attempting again.

b) In select apps, open windows manifest as thumbnails positioned near the lower edge of the screen. A simple touch on any thumbnail seamlessly transitions its contents into the current full-screen window. When utilizing Split View, tap the icon··· at the top of an open app to unveil all its active windows.

Creating New Windows within an App

1) When all open windows within an app are displayed as small previews at the screen's lower edge, observe the icon ╂. Tap it effortlessly to spawn a new window within the app.

2) In Split View mode, tap··· to showcase the app's open applications as miniatures, then touch ╂ to initiate the creation of a new window.

MASTERING PICTURE IN PICTURE

Unleash the complete capabilities of your iPad with Picture in Picture, a feature designed to elevate your multitasking capabilities to new heights. Seamlessly watch videos or engage in FaceTime conversations while effortlessly navigating through other apps. Here's strategies to optimize this innovative feature:

Activating Picture in Picture

1) While indulging in a video or FaceTime call, initiate Picture in Picture by tapping the designated icon or pressing the Home button (on iPads equipped with one).

Seamless Navigation

2) Watch in amazement as the video window gracefully scales down to an edge of your screen, allowing you to simultaneously access the Home Screen and other applications.

Optimizing the Video Window Effortlessly tailor your viewing experience with these intuitive actions:

3) Resize the video window to your liking by executing a pinch gesture. Pinch open to enlarge the window, or pinch closed to shrink it.

4) Tap the video window to reveal or conceal controls.

5) Customize the placement of the video window by effortlessly dragging it to a different edge of the screen.

6) When it's time to temporarily hide the video window, simply drag it off the left or right edge of the screen.

7) To bid farewell to the video window, tap .

8) Want to immerse yourself fully in the video again? Tap in the small video window to return to a full-screen experience.

MASTER MULTITASKING WITH STAGE MANAGER: REDEFINE YOUR WORKFLOW ON IPAD

Unlock the Power of Stage Manager to Streamline Multitasking Effortlessly

Discover a new frontier in productivity with Stage Manager, a revolutionary tool designed to elevate your multitasking experience on compatible iPad models. Effortlessly resize, rearrange, and organize windows to your liking, effortlessly navigating through multiple apps simultaneously.

Tailor your workspace to perfection by grouping apps according to specific tasks or projects. Utilizing Stage Manager, you have the freedom to craft your ideal layout, enabling seamless transitions between apps and maximizing efficiency.

Seamless Integration with External Displays

Link your iPad to an external display and seamlessly transition between screens with Stage Manager. Effortlessly drag windows between your iPad and external display, arranging them to match your workflow seamlessly.

Effortless Activation and Control

Toggle Stage Manager on or off with ease, allowing you to focus on what matters most: your work. When activated, Stage Manager intelligently positions your current app at the middle of the display, optimizing its size for enhanced productivity. Meanwhile, remaining active applications neatly align along the side, readily accessible for quick navigation.

Unlock the complete capabilities Stage Manager
Step into the future of multitasking by enabling Stage Manager on your iPad:

1. Access **Settings** > **Multitasking & Gestures**.
2. Simply tap the checkbox located below Stage Manager, and toggle on "Recent Apps."

Quick Access through Control Center

a) Access Stage Manager swiftly by opening **Control Center** and tapping the designated icon.

Seamless Multitasking with Multiple Windows

Utilizing Stage Manager, multitasking becomes intuitive and efficient. Consolidate applications for designated tasks or initiatives, and maintain their cohesion throughout your workflow. Effortlessly reposition, resize, and overlap windows to align with your unique work style.

1) Open an app and seamlessly integrate it with your current task by following these steps:

   a) Tap the icon located at the upper section of a window and select "Add Another Window." This action reveals all recent app windows, permitting you to pick the one you wish to add.

   b) Alternatively, touch and hold an app in the Recent Apps list, then move it to the current window in the middle of the screen. This action seamlessly incorporates the selected app into your existing workspace.

   c) Touch and hold an application in the Dock, then effortlessly drag it upward towards the middle of your screen. (**NOTE**: If the Dock isn't visible,

Slide upward from the screen's lower boundary to unveil it.)

d) Alternatively, access the Application Library icon (located at the rightmost position in the Dock). Long-press an application icon within the Application Library, then smoothly drag it from the library to the center of your screen.

2) **Effortlessly Navigate Multiple Apps**: Optimize your multitasking capabilities with these simple actions:

a) Resize any window by dragging from the corner marked with a dark curve. Alternatively, if you're using a mouse or trackpad, simply drag from any corner or edge of the panel to adjust its size to your preference.

b) Streamline your workspace by moving a window to the Recent Apps list. Tap the icon ••• situated at the upper section of the window, then select "Minimize" to seamlessly transition it to the list of recent apps.

c) Move a window by simply dragging from the upper section of the window.

d) Enlarge a window by tapping the icon°°° at the upper section of the window, then selecting "Enter Full Screen."

Maximize Your Workspace Efficiency

Boost your productivity with more screen space:

- On supported models, access **Settings**⚙ >then press **Display & Brightness**, tap **Display Zoom**, and then select **More Space** to increase pixel density. This option allows for optimal viewing of multiple app windows within Stage Manager or Split View.

Seamless App Navigation

Effortlessly switch between apps using Stage Manager's intuitive interface:

1) Access recent applications by selecting one from the list of recently used apps or by choosing an icon on the Dock.
2) When transitioning to another app, your current app or group smoothly transitions to the Recent apps list, seamlessly replaced by the app you've selected.

Additional App Switching Options

Explore alternative methods to alternate between applications:

a) Slide upwards from the lower of the display, then hold briefly in the middle to access recent apps and groups swiftly.
b) Glide your finger to the left or right across the screen's lower border.
c) Alternatively, Slide four or five fingers horizontally across the screen.

Customize Your Experience

Tailor your multitasking setup to your preferences:
1) Hide or show the recent apps list effortlessly:
   a) Access Control Center by swiping down from the screen's top right, long-press, then Press the tick symbol on the left-side of the image.

   b) Or, navigate to **Settings** > then press **Multitasking & Gestures**, press the checkbox underneath **Stage Manager** to activate it, then toggle **Recent App**s on or off.

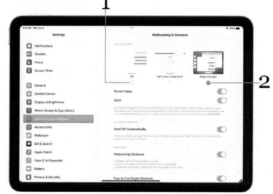

   1) *Switch off Stage Manager*
   2) *Switch on Stage Manager*

Pro Tip: Regain Control
a) Should the list of recent applications disappears when you bring a pane positioned too near to it, simply Drag from the screen's left boundary to make it reappear.

Closing Windows Made Simple

Clear clutter with ease by closing windows effortlessly:

1) Tap the icon ^{...} at the upper section of the window, then select "Close."
   a) If the window is part of a group of apps, it seamlessly disappears from the group.

Seamless Integration with External Displays

Maximize your workspace by extending your screen to an external screen:
1) Connect your iPad (supported models) to an external screen to seamlessly work across both screens.

Seamlessly Transfer Applications to External Displays

Enhance your productivity by moving applications across screens:
1) Begin by dragging from the top edge of the app window, then move it to the desired display.
2) Alternatively, drag the icon of the application you intend to shift to seamlessly transition it between displays.

UNLOCKING THE CAPABILITIES OF YOUR IPAD LOCK SCREEN

Unlocking Convenience at Your Fingertips
The iPad Lock Screen isn't just a gateway to your device; it's a powerhouse of efficiency waiting to be tapped into. Upon powering on or waking your iPad, this screen greets you with the essentials: time, date, and recent notifications. But its utility extends far beyond mere aesthetics. Here's how you can leverage its full potential effortlessly.

SEIZE CONTROL, EVEN WHEN LOCKED

From capturing spontaneous moments to swiftly toggling settings, the Lock Screen empowers you to take charge without having to unlock your iPad.

1) **Snap Away with Ease**: Swipe left to instantly access your Camera, ensuring you never miss a snapshot-worthy moment.

2) **Master Your Settings**: Simply slide downward from the upper-right edge to unveil the Control Center, your command center for toggling settings and accessing essential features.

3) **Stay Updated Effortlessly**: Slide upward from the center to catch up on earlier notifications without unlocking your iPad.

4) **Expand Your Horizons**: Swipe right to discover additional widgets, extending the functionality of your Lock Screen. These widgets aren't just for show; interact with them to complete tasks directly from the Lock Screen. For instance, mark off items within the Reminders widget or kickstart an episode within the Podcasts widget with a simple tap.

5) **Unleash Your Creativity**: On compatible models, tap your Apple Pencil on the Lock Screen to

seamlessly transition into drawing or note-taking mode. Every stroke and thought is securely stored in Notes for your convenience.

6) **Command Your Media**: Utilize the **media playback interface** displayed on the Lock Screen to manage your media playback effortlessly. Control the playback of media on your device with options to start, stop, go back, or skip ahead on your iPad without unlocking your device.

STAY INFORMED WITH NOTIFICATION PREVIEWS

To ensure you never miss important updates, Proceed with the following straightforward instructions:

1. Navigate to **Settings** > **Notifications**.
2. Tap on "Show Previews," then select "Always."

By enabling notification previews, you'll have access to crucial information right from your Lock Screen. Whether it's a snippet from a text message, a preview of an email, or details about upcoming calendar events, you'll stay informed at a glance.

TAKE COMMAND OF YOUR ENTERTAINMENT AND UPDATES

Your Lock Screen isn't just a static display; it's a hub of real-time updates and control. Here's how you can harness its power:

1) **Live Activities at Your Fingertips**: Experience live updates directly on your Lock Screen, from sports scores to order statuses, flight tracking, and media playback. Stay engaged and informed without unlocking your iPad.

2) **Effortless Media Management**: When enjoying music, movies, or other media on your iPad, utilize the playback controls in Now Playing on your Lock Screen. Play, pause, rewind, and fast-forward with ease, all from the convenience of your Lock Screen.

3) **Seamless Remote Control**: Extend your media control beyond your iPad. Control playback on compatible devices like your Apple TV or HomePod directly from your iPad Lock Screen, simplifying your entertainment experience.

MASTER QUICK ACTIONS ON YOUR IPAD

Unlocking Efficiency with Every Touch
Discover the power of swift actions at your fingertips, whether you're on the Home Screen, navigating Control Center, or immersed in your favorite apps.

Seamless Previews and Quick Access
In various contexts, the iPad empowers you to effortlessly preview content and access quick action menus with just a touch:

1) **Photos**: Simply Long-Press an image to preview it instantly, accompanied by a handy list of options for further actions.

2) **Mail**: Navigate through your messages with ease by touching and holding a message in your mailbox to preview its contents. Explore a range of options without needing to open the message fully.

3) **Home Screen**: Improve your browsing journey by briefly touching and holding an app icon to unveil a quick actions menu. Should the icons start to dance, simply press "Done" at the upper right or hit the Home button (for iPads equipped with one) and try again.

4) **Control Center**: Dive into Control Center and discover a realm of possibilities. Touch and hold items like Camera or brightness controls to reveal additional options, allowing for personalized adjustments on the fly.

5) **Lock Screen**: Stay connected and responsive even while your iPad remains in a secured state. Briefly touch and hold a notification to swiftly respond, ensuring you never miss a beat.

6) **Effortless Typing**: Elevate your typing experience by touching and holding the Space bar with one finger. Watch as your onscreen keyboard transforms into a trackpad, granting you precise cursor control with ease.

UNLEASH THE POWER OF SPOTLIGHT SEARCH ON YOUR IPAD

Effortless Exploration at Your Fingertips

Discover the remarkable capabilities of Spotlight Search on your iPad, allowing you to swiftly locate apps, contacts, and content across various applications. Delve into the depths of your device and beyond with ease, finding everything from stock updates to webpages and images in your photo library.

Tailored Results for Seamless Navigation

Spotlight Search isn't just about finding what you need; it's about finding it quickly and efficiently. Here's what you can expect:

1) **App and Content Search**: Effortlessly search for apps, contacts, and content within apps like Mail and Messages. With Live Text, even text within your photos becomes searchable, opening up an array of potential opportunities.

2) **Smart Suggestions and Updates**: Receive intuitive suggestions based on your app usage, ensuring that your search results are always relevant and up to date. Watch as the results dynamically update as you type, providing a seamless search experience.

3) **Top Hit Shortcuts for Quick Access**: Instantly access your most frequently used apps with Top Hit shortcuts. When searching for an app, convenient shortcuts to your next likely action appear, simplifying your navigation process.

CUSTOMIZE YOUR SEARCH EXPERIENCE

Tailor Spotlight Search to your preferences by choosing which apps you like to include in your search outcomes. Follow these instructions:

1. Navigate to **Settings** > then press **Siri & Search**.

2. Scroll down and select an app, then toggle "Show App in Search" on or off as desired.

NAVIGATE YOUR IPAD WITH EASE: MASTERING SEARCH

Effortless Exploration with a Swipe

Unlock the capabilities of your iPad's search feature, guiding you seamlessly through apps, websites, and actions with just a few touches. Here's strategies to optimize it:

1) **Access Search Anywhere:** Drag your finger downwards from the center of your Home or Lock Screens to unveil the search field.

2) **Find What You Need:** Enter your query into the search field, and let your iPad do the rest.

3) **Dive Into Actions:** Once you've initiated your search, explore a range of possibilities:

   a) **Quick Access to Apps**: Tap on the suggested application to access it instantly, saving you precious time.

   b) **Swift Actions at Your Fingertips**: From setting a timer to running a shortcut, take quick actions directly from the search results. Discover shortcuts tailored to your apps or create your own using the Shortcuts app for ultimate efficiency.

   c) **Browse Suggested Websites**: Tap on a suggested website to delve deeper into the information you seek.

   d) **Explore Search Suggestions**: Dive into search suggestions to uncover more information. Tap on a suggestion, then select a result to open it and gain further insights.

e) **Initiate a Fresh Search**: Ready to explore something new? Just select the ⊗ in the search field to start afresh.

CUSTOMIZE YOUR EXPERIENCE

Tailor your search experience to your preferences by turning off location-based suggestions:

1. Navigate to **Settings** ⚙ > then press **Privacy Security** > press **Location Services**.
2. Tap on "System Services" and toggle off "Suggestions & Search."

SEARCH LIKE A PRO: NAVIGATING WITHIN APPS

Unlocking the Depths of Your Applications
Discover the power of searching within your apps, allowing you to swiftly locate specific information or features. Whether you're exploring maps or diving into documents, here's strategies to optimize in-app search functionalities:

1) **Find What You Need Within Apps:** In many apps, you'll find a dedicated search field or button for easy access to search functionality. For instance, in the Maps application, you can search for specific locations to pinpoint your desired destination.
   a) **Navigate Within the App**: Just select the search field or button 🔍 within the app interface.
   b) **Swipe Down for Quick Access**: If you can't locate the search feature within the app, simply drag downwards from the upper edge of the screen in order to reveal the search option.

2) **Execute Your Search:** Once you've accessed the search functionality within the application, follow these steps:
   a) **Enter Your Query**: Type your search query into the designated field.
   b) **Initiate the Search**: Tap on the "Search" button to commence your search.

IMPROVE YOUR SEARCH RESULTS WITH DICTIONARIES

On your iPad, you can decide to augment your search capabilities by adding dictionaries. Here's how:

1. Navigate to **Settings** > **General** > **Dictionary**.
2. Choose from a selection of dictionaries available for integration into your searches.

MASTERING YOUR IPAD: AN IN-DEPTH MANUAL FOR ACCESSING KEY INFORMATION

EFFORTLESSLY MANAGE YOUR IPAD'S STORAGE

Discover Overall Storage Availability and App Usage
To check how much storage is available on your iPad and see the storage used by each app:

1. Access the **Settings** Application.
2. Navigate to **General**.
3. Select **iPad Storage**.

MONITOR BATTERY USAGE WITH EASE

Track Your Battery Usage and Optimize Performance

To view battery usage details, including the time elapsed since your iPad was last charged and usage by app:

1. Access the **Settings** Application.
2. Tap on **Battery**.

Here, you can also choose to display the battery level as a percentage and toggle Low Power Mode on or off.

KEEP TABS ON YOUR CELLULAR DATA

View and Control Your Cellular Data Usage

For those using iPad models with cellular capabilities:

1. Access the **Settings** Application.
2. Go to **Cellular Data**.

ACCESS COMPREHENSIVE DETAILS PERTAINING TO YOUR IPAD

Detailed Device Information at Your Fingertips

To find detailed Details Pertaining to Your iPad:

1. Access the **Settings** Application.
2. Navigate to **General**.
3. Select **About**.

Here, you can view essential details such as:
a) Device Name
b) iPadOS Software Version
c) Model Name
d) Component and Serial Identifiers (select the component ID to view the model number)
e) Serial Number

f) Network Status (applicable to Wi-Fi + Mobile Network versions)
g) Count of Songs, Videos, Photos, and Apps
h) Total Capacity and Available Storage Space
i) Carrier Details (applicable to Wi-Fi + Mobile Network versions)
j) Cellular Data Number (applicable to Wi-Fi + Mobile Network versions)
k) Wi-Fi and Bluetooth® Addresses
l) IMEI (International Mobile Equipment Identity) (applicable to Wi-Fi + Mobile Network versions)
m) ICCID (Integrated Circuit Card Identifier) for GSM Networks (applicable to Wi-Fi + Mobile Network versions)
n) MEID (Mobile Equipment Identifier) for CDMA Networks (applicable to Wi-Fi + Mobile Network versions)
o) Modem Firmware Version

To copy any of the serial numbers or other identifiers, simply Long-press the respective identifier until the option to "Copy" appears.

Access Legal & Regulatory Information

For legal notices, license details, warranty information, and RF exposure guidelines:

1. Access the **Settings** Application.
2. Navigate to **General**.
3. Select **Legal & Regulatory**.

MANAGE DIAGNOSTIC INFORMATION

Gain control over diagnostic and usage data transmission:

1. Access the **Settings** Application.

2. Go to **Privacy & Security**.
3. Choose **Analytics & Improvements**.

By providing performance and utilization information, you contribute to Apple's efforts to enhance products and services. Rest assured, this data is anonymized and does not personally identify you, although it might encompass positional details.

MASTERING MOBILE NETWORK CONFIGURATION FOR YOUR IPAD (WI-FI + CELLULAR VARIANTS)

Seamlessly Oversee your mobile data usage

Unlock the complete capabilities your iPad's cellular capabilities by activating cellular data service, toggling cellular service on or off, and customizing which applications and services utilize cellular data. Plus, discover how to adjust your data plan with certain carriers for maximum flexibility.

Continue to engage with Your Mobile Provider

For help with cellular services and billing questions, contact Your Mobile Provider. They offer expert support and personalized assistance to meet your needs.

Understand Cellular Data Usage

Keep an eye on your iPad's status bar to easily identify when you're linked to the internet through the mobile data network. When Cellular Data is enabled, certain activities like email, web browsing, and push notifications utilize cellular data. Be mindful that engaging in data-intensive activities may result in carrier charges.

Note on Wi-Fi + Cellular Models
While Wi-Fi + Cellular models offer robust cellular data transmission capabilities, they do not support traditional cellular phone service. Instead, leverage features like Wi-Fi Calling in conjunction with an iPhone for making phone calls on your iPad.

UPGRADE YOUR IPAD EXPERIENCE: INTEGRATE A CELLULAR PLAN

Effortlessly Activate a Cellular Plan
If you've already configured a mobile data plan on your iPad, simply navigate to **Settings** > Next, select **Cellular**, choose **Add a New Plan**, and adhere to the prompts displayed on your screen to effortlessly complete the setup.

OVERSEE YOUR MOBILE DATA ACCOUNT WITH EASE

Take control of the consumption of your mobile data by accessing your account settings:

1. Access the Settings Application.
2. Go to **Cellular Data**.
3. Tap on **Manage [account name]** or **Carrier Services** to view or modify your account details.

OPTIMIZE CELLULAR DATA SETTINGS FOR BEST PERFORMANCE

Adjust your iPad's cellular data options to match your preferences and requirements:

1) Enable or disable Cellular Data by navigating to **Settings** > then select **Cellular**.
2) For advanced options, navigate to **Settings** >then press **Cellular** > press **Cellular Data Options**.
3) Here, you can:
   a) **Activate Low Data Mode to conserve cellular usage:** This setting suspends automatic downloads and secondary processes whenever your iPad isn't connected to Wi-Fi, helping to extend battery life and optimize performance.
   b) **Activate or Deactivate Data Roaming**: Enable Data Roaming to access the internet via a cellular data network when outside your carrier's coverage area. Switch it off to prevent incurring roaming fees while abroad.

Boost Data Speeds with LTE

Maximize data performance by toggling LTE on or off, depending on your iPad model, carrier, and region:

a) **Turn LTE On or Off**: Activate LTE to enjoy faster data loading speeds and smoother online experiences.

Optimize 5G Connectivity

For models that support 5G networks, unlock advanced Functions to improve your browsing experience:

a) **Enable Smart Data Mode**: Enhance battery life by selecting 5G Auto under Voice & Data. Your iPad smartly switches back to LTE when 5G speeds aren't significantly faster.

b) **Enhance Video and FaceTime Quality**: Opt for Allow More Data on 5G under Data Mode to enjoy higher-quality video streaming and FaceTime calls on 5G networks.

EFFORTLESSLY SHARE YOUR CELLULAR CONNECTION

Turn your iPad into a Personal Hotspot and share your cellular internet connection effortlessly:

1. Access to **Settings** > **Cellular** and switch on **Cellular Data**.
2. Tap on **Set up Personal Hotspot** and follow the prompts outlined in the screen to get started.

TAKE CONTROL OF YOUR APP AND SERVICE CELLULAR DATA USAGE

Customize Cellular Data Access for Apps and Services

Tailor your iPad's cellular data usage by managing access for individual apps and services:

1. Navigate to **Settings** > then press **Cellular Data**.
2. Enable or disable cellular data for specific applications or services, like Maps or others Wi-Fi Assist, that utilizes cellular data.

Ensure Optimal Connectivity with Wi-Fi Assist

Stay connected seamlessly with Wi-Fi Assist, which automatically switches to cellular network when Wi-Fi is unreliable:

a) **Wi-Fi Assist**: Enabled by default, Wi-Fi Assist boosts your signal by switching to cellular data if Wi-Fi quality is subpar. Keep in mind that this may result in increased cellular data usage, potentially leading to Extra fees contingent upon your mobile data agreement.

Protect the consumption of your mobile data by locking your SIM card utilizing a Personal Identification Number (PIN):

1) **Secure Your SIM Card**: Safeguard your device and prevent unauthorized use of your SIM card by configuring a PIN. Whenever you power cycle your device or remove the SIM card, it automatically locks, requiring you to enter your PIN for access.

OPTIMIZING YOUR IPAD SETTINGS FOR TRAVEL

Airplane Mode: Your Travel Companion
When embarking on a journey with your iPad, ensure your settings align with airline regulations. Many airlines permit the use of iPads in flight if you activate airplane mode. In this mode, Wi-Fi and Bluetooth® are initially disabled, blocking FaceTime calls and other wireless features. However, you can still enjoy music, games, videos, and offline applications without any issues.

Minimizing Cellular Charges Abroad
For Wi-Fi + Cellular models, it's essential to configure settings that mitigate unexpected data charges while traveling. Explore the option to adjust your cellular data settings on your iPad to optimize connectivity and control expenses efficiently.

Seamless Connectivity Anywhere

When journeying abroad, streamline your connectivity by considering local cellular service options directly from your iPad (compatible with Wi-Fi + Cellular versions featuring Touch ID or Face ID). This convenient feature empowers you to stay connected effortlessly, enhancing your travel experience.

Activating Airplane Mode: A Simple Guide

Quick Access via Control Center

To swiftly enable flight mode on your iPad, simply launch the **Control Center** and Select the flight mode symbol ✈. This action instantly disables Wi-Fi, Bluetooth®, and cellular connections, indicated by the flight mode symbol in the notification area.

1) Switch on airplane Mode

Alternate Method: Settings Navigation

Alternatively, navigate to Settings ⚙ to toggle flight mode on or off. Upon activation, the Flight Mode icon ✈

will be clearly visible in the status bar, thereby adhering to airline rules and regulations.

Using Bluetooth or Wi-Fi in Airplane Mode

If permitted by your airline, Wi-Fi or Bluetooth can still be utilized even in airplane mode. Adhere to these guidelines:

1. Access **Control Center** and then enable airplane mode.

2. Hit the Wi-Fi 📶 or Bluetooth icon 🔵 to enable the respective feature.

1) *Switch on Wi-Fi*
2) *Switch on Bluetooth*

Remembering Your Preferences

If you enable Wi-Fi or Bluetooth while in flight mode, they may remain active the next time you engage airplane mode. For switching off Wi-Fi or Bluetooth during airplane mode, access the Control Center again and tap the respective icons 📶 or 🔵.

1) *Switch off Wi-Fi in flight mode*
2) *Switch off Bluetooth in flight mode*

CHAPTER 4: PERSONALIZE YOUR IPAD

UNLOCKING PERSONALIZATION: MASTERING IPAD SOUND SETTINGS

Customize and Control Your iPad's Audio Experience
In the bustling world of technology, tailoring your device to your preferences enhances the experience. One fundamental aspect of personalization lies in managing the sounds emitted by your iPad. Whether you seek tranquility during focused work hours or wish to infuse a touch of personality into your device, Becoming proficient in sound customization empowers you to sculpt your digital ambiance effortlessly.

Soothing Silence: The Power of Sound Control
In the realm of iPad customization, the ability to tweak sound settings reigns supreme. Utilizing just a handful of straightforward maneuvers within your device's settings, you can effortlessly alter or silence the sounds accompanying incoming calls, text messages, emails, reminders, and various notifications. Embracing tranquility is as easy as activating the **Do Not Disturb** feature, temporarily hushing all incoming calls, alerts, and sound effects with a mere tap.

CRAFTING YOUR AUDIO OASIS: SETTING SOUND OPTIONS

Delving deeper into the auditory realm of your iPad, the avenue to fine-tune your sound preferences unveils itself through the Settings menu. Adhere to these guidelines to navigate this realm:

1. Access **Settings** > **Sounds**.
2. Slide the volume control to set the desired level for the ringer and alerts, granting you control over the auditory prominence of your device.
3. Explore further by tapping on Ringtone and other options, granting you the freedom to select personalized sounds for your ringtone and alert tones, infusing your device with your unique sonic identity.

Moreover, the journey towards tailored audio experiences extends beyond generic settings. Explore the domain of individualized sounds for specific contacts within your device's **Contacts** app . By tapping into the intricate details of your contacts, you can assign distinct ringtones and text tones, adding a personalized touch to your communication experience.

SILENCING YOUR IPAD'S SYMPHONY

Unleash Peace with a Simple Gesture
In the bustling cacophony of modern life, finding moments of tranquility can be a challenge. Yet, with your iPad at your side, serenity is just a tap away. Enter the realm of silence by Becoming proficient in temporarily silencing incoming calls, notifications, and auditory cues.

A Quiet Oasis: Navigating the Silence

1. **Access Control Center**: Journey into the heart of your iPad's interface and open Control Center, your gateway to tranquility.

2. **Tap into Focus**: Within Control Center, locate and tap into the domain of Focus, where distractions dissipate and focus reigns supreme.
3. **Initiate Do Not Disturb**: With a simple tap, invoke the power of Do Not Disturb, temporarily silencing the clamor of incoming calls, notifications, and auditory cues.

Pro Tip: Stay In Tune with Expectations

In the event that silence reigns when you anticipate a symphony of notifications, fear not. Navigate back to Control Center and verify that Do Not Disturb hasn't stealthily claimed dominion over your iPad. A quick glance at the status of the Do Not Disturb button 🌙 can unveil the culprit, allowing you to restore harmony with a simple tap.

CRAFT YOUR UNIQUE IPAD LOCK SCREEN EXPERIENCE

Harness the capabilities of Personalization
Unlocking your iPad isn't just about getting to your apps; it's a chance to make a statement. You have the ability to enhance your Lock Screen with personality, style, and functionality, all in a few simple steps. Let's dive into the world of custom Lock Screens and unleash your creativity!

Tailoring Your Lock Screen

You're not limited to a generic Lock Screen anymore. With your iPad, you can mold it to reflect your tastes and preferences effortlessly. Whether it's a striking wallpaper, a cherished photo, or a subtle font change, the possibilities are endless.

CREATING YOUR OWN LOCK SCREEN

1. Hold down on the Lock Screen until the options to Customize and emerge at the lower edge of your screen. If they don't show up, simply hold down again and input your passcode.

2. Tap to initiate a new Lock Screen creation. To tweak an existing one, swipe to your desired screen, tap **Customize**, then **Lock Screen**.

3. When crafting a new Lock Screen, choose from a variety of wallpaper preferences to set the mood. For a more personalized touch, explore the Photos or Photo Shuffle features to elevate your Lock Screen with cherished memories.

4. **Revamp Your Time Display**: Your Lock Screen's time display isn't just functional; it's an opportunity for personalization. Tap on the time to unlock a realm of font, color, and style choices. With a simple drag of the slider, you can modify the weight of the font to

match your preferences, offering a tailored touch to your device.

5. **Infuse Your Lock Screen with Widgets**: Transform your Lock Screen into an information hub with widgets that deliver today's headlines, weather updates, and upcoming calendar events right at your fingertips. To add widgets, simply tap on "Add Widgets" or the date. In landscape mode, opt for the left side to integrate widgets seamlessly. In portrait mode, explore below the time for widget placement. For added flexibility, consider placing widgets above the time as well.

6. **Finalize Your Lock Screen Masterpiece**: Once you've curated your Lock Screen elements to perfection, it's time to seal the deal. Tap "Add" or "Done," then select your preferred option: "Set as Wallpaper Pair" to apply the changes to both Lock Screen and Home Screen, or "Customize Home Screen" to fine-tune your Home Screen appearance. Dive into a spectrum of choices—from wallpaper colors to custom photos—and even experiment with blurring effects to ensure your apps pop against the background.

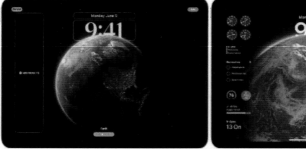

UNLEASH THE COMPLETE CAPABILITIES YOUR LOCK SCREEN PHOTO

When you opt for a personalized photo to grace your Lock Screen, you open the door to a realm of customization options. Elevate your Lock Screen experience by exploring these simple yet powerful tweaks:

1. **Reposition with Precision:** Don't settle for a static image. With a pinch and a drag, you can effortlessly reposition your chosen photo to ensure it captures the essence of your vision. Zoom in to focus on the finer details, drag utilizing two fingers to shift its position, and seamlessly zoom out to admire your masterpiece in its entirety.

2. **Experiment with Photo Styles:** Inject personality into your Lock Screen with a variety of photo styles at your disposal. Slide left or right to explore different styles, each accompanied by complementary color filters and fonts. From classic elegance to vibrant modernity, find the perfect style that resonates with your aesthetic sensibilities.

3. **Embrace Multilayered Magic:** Take your Lock Screen to the subsequent level with a mesmerizing multilayered effect, adding depth and dimension to your chosen photo. If your picture has the capacity for layering—like landscapes, portraits, or panoramic views—activate this feature by tapping on the icon ⊙ at the bottom right and choosing **Depth Effect**. Witness your photo come to life as it seamlessly integrates with the interface, offering a captivating visual experience.

   Note: The multilayered effect is accessible on supported models. Keep in mind that layering may not be feasible if the subject is too high or too low, or if it obstructs too much of the clock.

4. **Engage with Live Photos:** Transform your Lock Screen experience with Live Photos, adding a touch of motion and vitality to your device. Simply select a Live Photo and tap ▶ at the lower left to unleash its dynamic potential. Watch as your Lock Screen springs to life with captivating movement whenever your device wakes up.

5. **Personalize with Photo Shuffle:** Unleash the element of surprise with Photo Shuffle, allowing your Lock Screen to showcase a rotating gallery of your favorite images. Take control of the shuffle frequency by tapping ⊙ and selecting your desired option, ensuring a fresh visual experience every time you unlock your device.

Pro Tip: Seamless Integration with Your Photo Library

For added convenience, directly incorporate photos from your library onto your Home Screen and Lock Screen. Navigate to the **Photos** app ❋, select your desired image, and tap ⬆. Scroll down to "Use as Wallpaper," tap "Add," and choose whether to display it on both your Home and Lock Screens.

MAXIMIZE YOUR PRODUCTIVITY WITH LINKED FOCUS ON YOUR LOCK SCREEN

Integrating Focus into your Lock Screen empowers you to stay on track and maintain productivity amidst a sea of distractions. Follow these straightforward steps to

128

seamlessly link a Focus to your Lock Screen and experience uninterrupted concentration:

1. **Access Lock Screen Customization:** Begin by holding down on your Lock Screen till the "Customize" button materializes near the screen's bottom. This step sets the stage for tailoring your Lock Screen experience to suit your productivity needs.

2. **Explore Focus Options:** Navigate to the lower edge of your wallpaper and tap on "Focus" to reveal a spectrum of Focus options tailored to different contexts. Whether it's "Do Not Disturb," "Personal," "Sleep," or "Work," choose the Focus that aligns with your current task or objective.

Note: *If the "Focus" option isn't immediately visible, head over to Settings* *to configure your Focus preferences.*

3. **Select and Activate Your Focus:** Once you've identified the ideal Focus for your Lock Screen, simply press it and confirm your selection. Your Lock Screen is now synced with your chosen Focus, ensuring that its settings seamlessly integrate into your device usage.

POLISH YOUR LOCK SCREEN TO EXCELLENCE

After you've designed your unique Lock Screen, the path to customization continues. Adhere to these instructions to effortlessly edit or switch between Lock Screens, tailoring your device to match your evolving preferences:

Editing Your Lock Screen:

1. Begin by holding down on your Lock Screen till the options for "Customize" and ⊕emerge near the screen's bottom. If they don't initially appear, repeat the process and input your passcode if prompted.
2. Navigate to the particular screen you want to alter, then hit 'Customize' and subsequently 'Lock Screen'.
3. Delve into the specifics by tapping on the time, which lets you modify the font, style, and color according to your preference.
4. Enhance functionality by incorporating widgets displaying today's headlines, weather updates, and upcoming calendar events. Simply tap "Add Widgets" or the date to integrate these features seamlessly.
5. Once satisfied with your edits, tap "Add" or "Done," then proceed to either "Set as Wallpaper Pair" to apply changes to both Lock Screen and Home Screen, or "Customize Home Screen" for further refinement.

SWITCHING BETWEEN LOCK SCREENSS:

1. Long-press your Lock Screen till the "Customize" button surfaces near the screen's bottom, signaling that you're ready to switch between your personalized Lock Screens effortlessly.
2. Swipe through your Lock Screens until you find the one you wish to use, then simply tap on it.

Note: If a Lock Screen is linked to a specific Focus, switching to another Lock Screen also changes your Focus accordingly.

STREAMLINE YOUR LOCK SCREEN COLLECTION

If you find yourself with Lock Screens you no longer need, it's a breeze to tidy up your selection:

1. Keep pressing your Lock Screen until the "Customize" button emerges near the screen's bottom.
2. Swipe to navigate to the Lock Screen you like to bid farewell to, then swipe up on the screen to reveal additional options. Tap 🗑, followed by "Delete This Wallpaper" to remove it from your collection.

Pro Tip: For seamless Lock Screen transitions, consider automating the process by linking specific Lock Screens to corresponding Focus modes. With this setup, switching to a particular Focus automatically switches your Lock Screen, ensuring a seamless and tailored experience.

REVAMP YOUR IPAD'S APPEARANCE WITH FRESH WALLPAPER

Harness the capabilities of Personalization

REVAMP YOUR DEVICE'S AESTHETIC

1) Begin by navigating to **Settings** ⊚ on your iPad.
2) Proceed downward and select Wallpaper, followed by Add New Wallpaper.
   a) This action will unveil a captivating gallery of wallpapers for your perusal.
3) Explore your options:
   a) Tap on the different buttons at the upper section of the gallery to experiment with various themes such as Photos, Photo Shuffle, Live Photo, and more.
   b) Dive into the featured sets like Collections, Astronomy, or Weather for a curated selection.
4) Should you opt for a Photo or Photo Shuffle, delve deeper into customization by referring to our section on Customizing your Lock Screen photo.
5) After locating the perfect wallpaper, tap Add, then choose from the following options:
   a) Designate as Matching Backgrounds
   b) Customize Home Screen
   c) Feel free to mix and match until you achieve the desired ambiance.

Bonus Tip: Elevate your wallpaper experience by setting up automatic changes. Proceed to the Shortcuts app and create a personal automation. Schedule it to your liking and integrate the Set Wallpaper action for seamless transitions.

BECOMING PROFICIENT IN ADJUSTING SCREEN BRIGHTNESS AND COLOR ON YOUR IPAD

Unlock the complete capabilities Visual Comfort
Modifying the brightness and color of your iPad display is a breeze, offering you optimal viewing comfort tailored to your preferences. Whether you're looking to conserve battery life or enhance readability, you're in control.

FINE-TUNE BRIGHTNESS MANUALLY

To effortlessly tweak the brightness levels of your screen, test out one of these simple methods:

1) Swipe downwards from the top right to access **Control Center**, then adjust the brightness slider ☀ to your desired level.

2) Access **Settings** ⚙, tap on **Display & Brightness**, and slide the brightness bar to achieve the perfect luminosity.

LET YOUR IPAD ADAPT AUTOMATICALLY

For a hands-free approach, enable your iPad to intelligently adjust its brightness based on ambient light conditions. Here's how:

1. Head to **Settings** ⚙, then tap on **Accessibility**.
2. Pick **Display & Text Size** and switch on the **Auto-Brightness** feature.

ENHANCE YOUR IPAD USAGE WITH DARK MODE

Enhance Comfort in Low-Light Settings. Embrace the Dark Side
Dark Mode offers a sleek, subdued color palette for your entire iPad interface, making it ideal for nighttime browsing or reading without disturbing others nearby.
Toggle Dark Mode with Ease

You have multiple options to activate or deactivate Dark Mode effortlessly:

1) Access Control Center by swiping down from the screen's top right, long-press the brightness control , then hit the Dark Mode icon to toggle it on or off.

2) Alternatively, head to **Settings**, choose **Display & Brightness**, and pick **Dark** to enable **Dark Mode** or **Light** to revert to the standard mode.

AUTOMATE DARK MODE FOR SEAMLESS TRANSITION

Streamline your experience by scheduling Dark Mode to activate automatically at night or according to a custom schedule:

1) Navigate to **Settings** and pick **Display & Brightness**.

2) Activate the **Automatic** feature, then delve into **Options** to refine your settings.

3) Choose the preset Sunset to Sunrise timetable or create a Custom Schedule tailored to align with your daily activities.

a) If you opt for Custom Schedule, simply tap the options to set the specific times for Night Shift activation and deactivation.
b) Alternatively, picking Sunset to Sunrise allows your iPad to intelligently adjust Night Shift based on your location and the time of day.

ACTIVATE NIGHT SHIFT AT YOUR CONVENIENCE

Manually toggle Night Shift on or off whenever the need arises, especially when you find yourself in dimly lit environments during the day.

1) Access Control Center by swiping down from the screen's top right, press and hold the brightness control, then hit the **Night Shift** icon to enable or disable it.

AUTOMATE YOUR VISUAL COMFORT

For a seamless transition, schedule Night Shift to automatically adjust your display's color temperature to a warmer hue at night:

1. Access **Settings**, then select **Display & Brightness** followed by **Night Shift**.
2. Enable the **Scheduled** option to activate automatic adjustments according to your preferred timing.
3. Assume command of your Night Shift experience by adjusting the color balance to suit your visual needs. Simply slide the Color Temperature bar to the warmer or cooler end of the spectrum for optimal comfort.

Customize Your Night Shift Schedule

1) Choose your preferred schedule setting:

a) Opt for the predefined Sunset to Sunrise schedule or craft a Custom Schedule tailored to your routine.
b) If you select Custom Schedule, tap into the options to set specific activation and deactivation times.
c) Alternatively, Sunset to Sunrise intelligently adapts Night Shift customized to your geographic setting and time, ensuring seamless transitions.

Stay Informed: Location Services Requirements

Note: If you disabled Location Services or Setting Time Zone, the Sunset to Sunrise option may not be accessible. Ensure Location Services are enabled in **Settings** > then press **Privacy & Security** for uninterrupted functionality.

ILLUMINATE YOUR ENVIRONMENT WITH TRUE TONE

For supported models, True Tone offers automatic adjustments to match your display's color and intensity with ambient lighting.
1) Activate or deactivate True Tone effortlessly:
    a) Access Control Center by swiping down from the screen's top right, Long-press the brightness control, then hit the True Tone icon to toggle it on or off.

    b) Alternatively, navigate to **Settings** > press **Display & Brightness** and switch **True Tone** according to your preference.

MASTERING TEXT CUSTOMIZATION ON YOUR IPAD: EASY STEPS FOR OPTIMAL VIEWING

Take Control of Your Display: Customize Text Size and Zoom Settings

Enhance your iPad experience by effortlessly adjusting text size and zoom settings to suit your preferences. Whether your goal is to enhance legibility, highlight text with bold formatting for impact, or enlarge the entire display, these straightforward instructions will enable you to operate your device effortlessly.

ENLARGE FONT SIZE FOR ENHANCED CLARITY

1. **Navigate to Settings**: Locate the **Settings** application on your iPad's main display and press to open.
2. **Access Display & Brightness**: Within Settings, select "Display & Brightness" to access a range of display customization options.
3. **Adjust Text Size**: Tap on "Text Size" and use the slider to effortlessly adjust text size to your preference. Slide left to decrease, or right to enlarge text size until it's just right for you.

MAKE TEXT STAND OUT WITH BOLD FORMATTING

1. **Find Your Settings**: Head back to the **Settings** application on your iPad's main display.
2. **Bolden Your Text**: Within "Display & Brightness," toggle on the "Bold Text" option to instantly make your text more prominent and easier to spot.

MAGNIFY YOUR SCREEN WITH DISPLAY ZOOM

Experience enhanced visibility across your entire iPad screen with the Display Zoom feature, available on supported models.

1. **Access Settings**: Return to the **Settings** application ⊚ once more.
2. **Activate Display Zoom**: Under "Display & Brightness," select "Display Zoom" to unlock screen magnification capabilities.
3. **Choose More Space**: Tap on "More Space" to magnify the screen for a clearer view of content.
4. **Confirm Your Selection**: Tap "Done," then select "Use More Space" to apply your chosen zoom settings.

STAND OUT: CHANGE YOUR IPAD'S NAME WITH EASE

Make your iPad truly your own by customizing its name. Whether it's for iCloud, AirDrop, Bluetooth®, or more, a unique name adds a personal touch to your device.

1. **Navigate to Settings**: Begin by touching the **Settings** app icon ⊚.
2. **Access General Settings**: Within Settings, find and press on "General."
3. **Find Your iPad's Name**: Tap on "About," then select "Name."
4. **Choose a New Name**: Tap the current name, enter your desired name, and hit "Done" to finalize your selection.

STAY IN SYNC: ADJUST DATE AND TIME SETTINGS

Ensure your iPad reflects the correct date and time, whether you're at home or on the go. Whether you favor automatic updates or manual tweaks, maintaining your device's clock precision is crucial.

1) **Access Settings:** Initiate the **Settings** application on your iPad.

2) **Navigate to General Settings:** Scroll down and select 'General'.

3) **Access Date & Time**: Within General settings, tap on "Date & Time."

4) **Select Your Preference**: Toggle on "Set Automatically" to allow your iPad to sync with network time and adjust based on your geographic setting. On the other hand, you can switch it off to modify the date and time settings by hand according to your preferences.

5) **Embrace the 24-Hour Clock: Opt for Military Time:** Switch to the 24-hour time format for a streamlined display of hours ranging from 0 to 23. Note that this feature may not be accessible across various international locales.

   a) **Access Date & Time Settings**: Navigate to **Settings** > press **General** > **Date & Time**.

   b) **Toggle Set Automatically Off**: Turn off "Set Automatically" to manually adjust the date and time settings.

   c) **Modify Time Display**: Change the displayed time to reflect the 24-hour format as per your preference.

Pro Tip: For further customization, explore options to alter the font color and style of the clock on your iPad's Lock Screen.

ENHANCE MULTICULTURAL EXPERIENCE: CHANGE LANGUAGE AND REGION SETTINGS

Ensure your iPad aligns with your language preferences and geographic location. Whether you're traveling abroad or settling into a new region, adjust the language and region settings effortlessly.

1) **Access Language & Region Settings**: Open **Settings** and navigate to **General > Language & Region**.

2) **Customize your language settings and location details**: Set your preferred language for iPad usage and choose your desired form of address (feminine, masculine, or neutral). Enable "Share with All Apps" for a personalized experience across various applications.

3) **For Region Settings:** Access **Settings**, then tap on **General > Language & Region** to choose your preferred region, this ensures you receive correct information and features specific to your location.

4) **Calendar Format:** Adjust your calendar format to match your preferred style for displaying dates.

5) **Temperature Unit**: Choose between Celsius or Fahrenheit to view temperature readings in your preferred unit.

6) **Measurement System**: Select your preferred measurement system—metric, US customary, or UK imperial—to ensure consistency in measurements.
7) **Commencement of the Weekly Calendar:** Set the Commencement of the Weekly Calendar: according to your cultural or personal preference.

Tap into the potential of Live Text
Unlock the ability to interact with text within images seamlessly with Live Text. Copy, search, or take action on text directly from images with this innovative feature.
a) **Enable Live Text**: Look for Live Text functionality to be integrated within various apps and contexts on your iPad.

Expand Your Language Options
Broaden your communication horizons by adding keyboards for additional languages.
b) **Add Keyboards**: Access **Settings** > then press **General** > **Keyboard** > **Keyboards**, then tap "Add New Keyboard" to select and install keyboards for other languages.

MASTERING HOME SCREEN ORGANIZATION: SIMPLIFY YOUR IPAD EXPERIENCE

STREAMLINE YOUR APPS WITH FOLDERS

Effortlessly organize your applications into folders to optimize your Home Screen layout and streamline navigation.

Creating Folders: A Step-by-Step Guide

1) **Enter Edit Mode**: Long-press any application icon on your Home Screen until they start jiggling, then tap "Edit Home Screen."

2) **Initiate Folder Creation**: Move an application icon onto another app icon to generate a folder.

3) **Add More Apps**: Continue dragging additional apps into the folder to consolidate similar apps together. You can have multiple pages of apps within a single folder.

4) **Personalize Folder Names**: To rename a folder, long-press it, then tap "Rename" and input a fresh name that reflects the contents of the folder.

   a) **Tip**: If the apps start jiggling unintentionally, press the Home Screen background to reset and try again.

5) **Finalize Your Changes**: Once you're satisfied with your folder organization, tap "Done" to exit Edit mode.

Deleting Folders: Cleaning Up Your Home Screen

To remove a folder, simply follow these steps:

a) **Open the Folder**: Tap on the folder to open it.

b) **Empty the Directory**: Relocate all applications from the directory until it's empty.

c) **Automatic Deletion**: The folder will be automatically deleted as soon as all applications have been are removed.

Note: While organizing your applications on the Home Screen enhances accessibility, it won't affect the organization of applications in the Application Library.

Enhance Accessibility: Move Apps with Ease

Make finding and accessing your favorite apps a breeze by seamlessly relocating them between folders and your Home Screen.

Moving Apps from Folders to Home Screen: A Quick Tutorial

1. **Access the Folder**: Navigate to the Home Screen page containing the folder housing the desired app. Tap the folder to open it.
2. **Enter Edit Mode**: Long-press the application icon within the folder until all apps start jiggling.
3. **Drag to Home Screen**: During the editing process, move the app icon from the folder onto the Home Screen, positioning it where you prefer for easy access.

Resetting Layout for a Fresh Start

If you're looking to revert to your iPad's original layout, adhere to these instructions:

1. **Access Settings**: Access the Settings Application ⚙ on your iPad.
2. **Navigate to Reset**: Scroll downwards and activate "General," then select "Reset."
3. **Restore Home Screen Layout**: Hit "Reset Home Screen Layout" to restore your Home Screen to its default configuration.

Upon resetting, any folders you've created will be removed, and your downloaded apps will be alphabetically ordered alongside pre-installed apps.

UNLOCK THE POWER OF YOUR IPAD: MASTERING WIDGETS

Maximize Your Productivity with Quick Glance Information

Understanding Widgets: Widgets are your personal dashboard on your iPad, providing instant access to crucial information such as headlines, Updates on the weather, reminders, battery level, and more. These are located in the Today View, but you can also place them on your Lock Screen or Home Screen for faster access.

Ease of Use: The charm of widgets is in their effortless interaction. Without needing to open individual apps, you can directly engage with widgets right from your Home or Lock Screens. Whether it's playing your favorite tunes, catching up on podcasts, browsing Safari, managing your smart home with HomeKit, or reaching out to contacts, widgets put functionality at your fingertips.

Adding Widgets to Your Home Screen:

1) Navigate to the page on your Home Screen where you wish to incorporate a widget.
2) Long press on any vacant section of the Home interface until the apps start to jiggle.
3) Tap the ⊕ symbol at the upper section of the screen to access the widget gallery.
4) Explore and Customize:
   a) Scroll through the widget gallery or use the search function to locate your desired widget. Tap on it, then slide left and right to preview

different size options. Each size offers varying information to suit your needs.

5) Adding to Your Screen:
   a) After locating the perfect fit, tap "Add Widget."
6) Positioning with Precision:
   a) While the apps continue to jiggle, drag the widget to your preferred location on the screen. Once satisfied, tap "Done."

1.   *The widgets can be saved on your Home screen*

Pro Tip: Unlock the Power of Smart Stacks:

a) Keep an eye out for the Smart Stack option (identified by dots). This dynamic set of widgets intelligently adjusts its display considering factors like location, time, and activity, ensuring you always have the most relevant information at your fingertips. To include a Smart Stack to your Home Screen, simply follow the same steps and swipe up and down to explore its contents.

Engage with Ease:

Interacting with widgets is a breeze, whether you're on your Home or Lock Screens. From marking off tasks in the Reminders widget to diving into a podcast episode with a single touch on the Play button in the Podcasts widget, or even illuminating your living room with a tap on the Home widget—everything is just a touch away, no need to launch the app.

Personalize Your Usage:

Adjust your widgets to your liking directly from your Home Screen. Interested in viewing the weather forecast for your locality or a different place? Just modify your Weather widget. Or perhaps you prefer a Smart Stack that adapts to your daily routine, location, and time of day automatically—customize it to your heart's content.

Editing Widgets on Your Home Screen:
1) Long press on the widget you like to edit to reveal the quick actions menu.
2) **Customize to Your Heart's Content:**
    a) Select "Edit Widget" or "Edit Stack" (for Smart Stacks), and explore the array of options at your fingertips.
    b) For Smart Stacks, toggle Smart Rotate or Widget Suggestions on or off, rearrange widgets within the stack by dragging, or remove unwanted widgets with a single touch on the negative indicator (−) found on the upper-left.
    c) Enabling Widget Suggestions ensures that relevant widgets for your frequently used apps seamlessly integrate into your Smart Stack based on your activity history, ensuring you have what you need as required.
3) **Final Touch:**
    a) Once you've tailored your widgets to perfection, tap "Done."

Bid Farewell to Unwanted Widgets:

1. Long-press on the widget you wish to bid adieu to, opening the quick actions menu.
2. Select "Remove Widget" or "Remove Stack," then confirm by tapping "Remove."

Discover Widgets with Ease in Today View:

To access your widgets in Today View, simply swipe right from the left edge of your Home Screen, then effortlessly scroll up and down to explore.

Unlock the Power of Widgets on Locked Screen:

If widgets are not readily available when swiping right on the Lock Screen, Adhere to these instructions to enable them:

1) Navigate to **Settings** .
2) Choose an option below that corresponds to your iPad model:
   a) Touch ID & Passcode
   b) Face ID & Passcode
   c) Passcode
3) Input your passcode.
4) Toggle on "Today View and Search" located below "Allow Access When Locked."

MASTERING YOUR IPAD'S HOME SCREEN: A COMPLETE GUIDE TO ORGANIZING APPS AND WIDGETS

Unlock the Power to Personalize Your Home Screen
Transforming Your Home Screen Experience: Your iPad's Home Screen is your virtual platform, where you have the liberty to rearrange apps and widgets based on

your personal choices. Whether you're looking to declutter, streamline your workflow, or simply give your Home Screen a fresh new look, the possibilities are endless.

Pro Tip: Optimize Your Focus: Streamline your productivity by organizing apps and widgets related to specific tasks or focus areas, such as work, entertainment, or fitness, onto dedicated Home Screen pages. This way, you can effortlessly switch between different focuses with a single swipe.

Step-by-Step Guide to Moving Apps and Widgets:

1) Start by touching and holding any app or widget on your Home Screen.
2) Tap "Edit Home Screen" when the items begin to jiggle.
3) The adventure begins! Move the application or widget to your desired location:
   a) Another spot on the same page
   b) A different Home Screen page: Simply move the application to the right-edge of your screen. It might take a moment, but once the new page appears, you'll see dots above the Dock indicating how many pages you have and which one you're currently viewing.

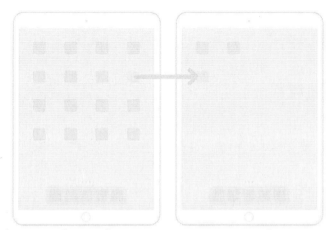

Top Tip: Docking for Convenience in a hurry? Quickly dock an app by dragging it to the lower part of your screen, right into the Dock.

4) **Finishing Touches:** Wrapping Up Your Edits Once you're satisfied with your adjustments, tap "Done" at the upper right edge to lock in your changes.

Returning to Your Original Configuration:

Resetting the Home Screen: Prepared for a fresh start? Follow these straightforward steps to revert your Home Screen and apps to their default arrangement:

1. Access **Settings** > then tap on **General** > tap on **Transfer or Reset iPad**.
2. Tap "Reset," then select "Reset Home Screen Layout," and confirm by tapping "Reset."

With this reset, any folders you've created will be removed, and your downloaded apps will be rearranged alphabetically, ensuring a clean slate for your Home Screen.

EFFORTLESSLY UNINSTALL OR ELIMINATE APPLICATIONS FROM YOUR IPAD

Discover the Simple Steps to Streamline Your iPad Experience

Removing or deleting applications from your iPad is a breeze, granting you the freedom to customize your device to fit your needs perfectly. The greatest advantage? Should you decide to backtrack, reinstalling your preferred apps is a breeze with just a handful of taps. Adhere to these instructions:

Uninstalling Applications from the Home Screen:

1. **Touch and Hold:** Find the application you like to erase on your Home Screen and touch and hold its icon until it begins to jiggle.

2. **Choose Your Option:** A menu will appear. Select "Remove App."

3. **Select Your Preference:** Decide whether to keep the app in your Application Library or delete it entirely from your iPad. Tap "Remove from Home Screen" to keep it in the library or "Delete App" to remove it completely.

Deleting Applications from the Application Library and Home Screen:

1. **Locate the Application:** Head to your App Library and locate the application you like to delete.

2. **Long Press:** Long-press the application icon until the options menu appears.

3. **Confirm Deletion:** Tap "Delete App" and then confirm by tapping "Delete" once more.

Remember, should you have a change of heart, you can easily re-download any apps you've deleted.

And there's more! Alongside third-party applications, you can also bid adieu to some of the built-in Apple apps that came with your iPad. Here's the list of these optional deletables:

1) Books
2) Calendar
3) Clock
4) Contacts (Note: Contact information remains accessible through Messages, Mail, FaceTime, and other apps. To entirely delete a contact, you'll require to restore Contacts.)
5) FaceTime (Note: In iPadOS 17.4 or later, removing FaceTime from your iPad will disable FaceTime calls and SharePlay sessions on your device until the application is redownloaded. See Make FaceTime calls on iPad.)
6) Files
7) Find My (Important: Removing this app doesn't disable location sharing or Find My for your device; it simply removes the ability to view locations in the Find My application on that device.)
8) Freeform
9) Health
10) Home
11) iTunes Store
12) Magnifier
13) Mail
14) Maps
15) Measure
16) Music
17) News
18) Notes
19) Photo Booth

20) Podcasts

21) Reminders

22) Shortcuts

23) Stocks

24) Tips

25) Translate

26) TV

27) Voice Memos

28) Weather

Keep in mind: Upon removing a pre-installed application from your Home Screen, you're also deleting all associated user information and setup documents. Additionally, removing built-in apps can potentially impact other system functionalities.

MAXIMIZE YOUR CONTROL: MASTERING AND PERSONALIZING THE CONTROL CENTER ON YOUR IPAD

Unlock the Power of Control Center for Instant Access to Essential Features and Apps

Control Center on your iPad is your one-stop hub for rapid retrieval of a range of essential controls and apps, from adjusting airplane mode and screen brightness to launching your flashlight or adjusting volume. Here's strategies to optimize it:

1. Long-tap to view Camera preferences

OPENING CONTROL CENTER:

To access Control Center, simply swipe downward from the upper-right edge of your iPad's screen. And when you're done, slide upwards from the lower to close it. It's that simple!

ACCESSING MORE CONTROLS:

But wait, there's more! Many controls in Control Center offer additional options. Just long-press a control to unlock its full potential. For example:

1) Press and keep your finger on the upper-left control cluster to reveal AirDrop options, enabling you to effortlessly share content with others.

2) Need to capture a moment? Long-press the camera control ⬚ to take a selfie, record a video, snap a photo, or even capture a slow-motion video, all without leaving Control Center.

ADDING AND ORGANIZING CONTROLS

Now, let's tailor Control Center to suit your needs perfectly:

1. Navigate to **Settings** > then press **Control Center on your iPad**.

2. For inserting or deleting controls, simply tap the or next to the control you want to customize.

3. For a personalized touch, rearrange controls by touching the ═ icon next to a control and dragging it to your preferred position.

TEMPORARILY DISCONNECT FROM WI-FI

In Control Center, a quick tap on the Wi-Fi icon disconnects you from your current network. To reconnect, simply tap it again. Need to check your network's name? Just Long-press the Wi-Fi icon 📶 for instant details. Plus, remember, disconnecting doesn't turn off Wi-Fi entirely, so AirPlay, AirDrop, and automatic network joining remain active. Should you wish to switch off Wi-Fi completely, head to **Settings** ⚙ > **Wi-Fi**. And when you're ready to reconnect, just tap the Wi-Fi icon 📶 in Control Center once more.

TEMPORARILY DISCONNECT FROM BLUETOOTH DEVICES

Similarly, in Control Center, a tap on the Bluetooth icon 🔵 temporarily disconnects your iPad from connected devices. To re-enable connections, tap the icon again. It's that easy! And just like with Wi-Fi, disconnecting from Bluetooth doesn't disable the feature entirely—location services and other Bluetooth-enabled functions remain active. To fully turn off Bluetooth, go to **Settings** ⚙ > tap on **Bluetooth** 🔵 and switch it off. To reconnect devices, simply tap the Bluetooth icon in the Control Center.

ADJUSTING CONTROL CENTER PERMISSIONS IN APPLICATIONS:

Interested in setting permissions for accessing the Control Center while using apps? Head to **Settings** ⚙ > press **Control Center** and then switch off "Access Within Apps" for included privacy and control.

UNVEILING THE MYSTERIES OF SCREEN ORIENTATION ON YOUR IPAD

Unlock the Capabilities of your iPad's Screen with Easy Orientation Controls

LOCK OR UNLOCK SCREEN ORIENTATION:

You have the ability to control how your iPad's screen behaves when you rotate the device. If you prefer to keep the screen in one orientation, simply lock it in place. Here's how:

1. Access the **Control Center** by dragging downwards from the upper-right edge of your iPad's screen.
2. Search for the icon that controls screen orientation lock. It resembles a lock encircled by a round arrow.

    By tapping this symbol, you can switch the screen orientation lock between active and inactive states. Once the screen orientation is secured, a diminutive lock symbol will become visible within the status bar located at the uppermost section of your iPad's screen, indicating that the orientation is fixed.

MASTER YOUR FOCUS: TAKING CHARGE OF NOTIFICATIONS

UNLOCK THE POWER OF NOTIFICATIONS ON YOUR IPAD

Notifications are your digital assistants, keeping you in the loop with what's new and important. Whether it's a missed call, a change in your schedule, or an update from your favorite app, notifications ensure you're always in sync.

Customize Your Notification Experience

Tailor your notifications to align with your tastes. Decide what matters most and receive notifications only for those crucial updates. With customizable settings, you're in control of how and when you receive notifications.

Maintain Order with the Notification Center

Your iPad's Notification Center is your go-to hub for staying organized. Unless you've muted notifications with a Focus mode or enabled Do Not Disturb, your iPad displays incoming notifications promptly. Missed a notification? No worries. It's securely stored in Notification Center for your convenience.

Access Your Notifications Anytime, Anywhere

Finding your notifications is a breeze. Simply Slide upward from the center of your Lock Screen to access Notification Center. Whether you're on the go or taking a break, staying informed is effortless with your iPad.

Swipe Down for Quick Access

On any screen other than your Lock Screen, simply swipe downward from the top center to reveal your notifications. Need to catch up on older notifications? Just scroll up to find what you missed.

Closing Notification Center

When you're done checking your notifications, closing Notification Center is just as easy. Slide upwards from the lower with a single finger, or hit the Home button on supported models to revert to your home screen seamlessly.

Efficiently Manage Grouped Notifications

Keeping track of multiple notifications is effortless with grouped notifications. Your iPad organizes them by app, simplify the process for you to stay organized and focused. Plus, some apps further organize notifications by topic or thread, ensuring you can manage them with precision.

Streamline Your Workflow

Expanding a group of notifications to view them individually is simple—just tap the group. Looking to reduce mess? Hit "Show Less" to collapse the group and keep a neat notification center.

Execute Swift Actions

When immediate response is required, press and hold a notification to see it and carry out the quick actions provided by the application. It's a seamless way to keep abreast of your duties without skipping a beat.

Effortlessly Navigate to Apps

When you receive a notification, accessing its corresponding app is a breeze. Just hit the notification, then tap "Open" to jump right into the app, allowing you to respond promptly and efficiently.

Stay Connected, Even on Lock Screen

Even if your iPad is in a locked state, staying connected is simple. Long-press the notification to quickly respond without unlocking your device, ensuring you never miss an important message or update.

Optimize Your Day with Scheduled Notifications

Take charge of your notifications and minimize distractions by scheduling them to be delivered as a summary. Custom-tailor your notification summary to include only what's essential, and choose the optimal time to receive it.

Personalized Notification Summary

Your notification summary is intelligently curated to suit your preferences and current activity. With priority-based ordering, the most relevant notifications are placed at the forefront, empowering you to stay focused and productive.

Enhance Focus with Scheduled Summary and Focus

Maximize your productivity by combining scheduled summary with Focus mode. Filter out distractions and notifications during your dedicated work or leisure time, ensuring uninterrupted focus and enhanced productivity.

Simple Setup for Scheduled Summary

Setting up your scheduled notification summary is quick and easy:

1. Access **Settings** > then press **Notifications** > press **Scheduled Summary**.
2. Toggle on **Scheduled Summary**.
3. Customize your summary by selecting the apps you wish to include, tailoring it to your unique requirements and tastes.
4. **Customize Your Notification Summary**: Assume command of your day by setting a specific time for your notification summary. Need multiple summaries throughout the day? No problem! Simply tap "Add Summary" to tailor your notifications to your schedule.
5. **Tailor Your Summary**: Ensure your notification summary includes all the apps you need by organizing them from A to Z. Easily toggle on the applications you like to include, ensuring you receive updates from your preferred sources.
6. **Streamline Your Notification Settings**: If you can't find an application in the A to Z list, it may need its notification permissions adjusted. Access **Settings** > **Notifications**, locate the app, and toggle on "Allow Notifications" to ensure it appears in your notification summary.

Efficiently Manage Notifications

When notifications pop up on your iPad, handling them is a breeze:

1) Need to respond to a notification when multitasking with another application? Just drag it downwards to

check, then flick upwards to close it without interrupting your workflow.

2) Keep your notification center clutter-free by swiftly clearing notifications. Slide left on a notification or a bundle of notifications, then touch "Clear" or "Clear All" to maintain a tidy workspace.

3) **Mute Notifications Temporarily**: When you need some uninterrupted focus, muting notifications for specific apps is the perfect solution. Simply swipe left on the notification or group of notifications, then press "Options," and select the duration—whether it's for an hour or a day. This ensures notifications are discreetly sent to Notification Center without disrupting your workflow.

4) **Restore Notifications**: Ready to re-engage with your notifications? It's as easy as sliding left on a notification in Notification Center, tapping "Options," and selecting "Unmute" to restore notifications to their original settings.

5) **Turn Off Notifications Completely**: For apps or notification groups that you no longer wish to receive notifications from, turning them off is a breeze. Slide left on the notification or group, tap "Options," and select "Turn Off" to stop notifications altogether.

6) **Customize Notification Display**: Tailor how notifications are displayed for individual apps to align with your tastes. Swipe left on a notification, tap "Options," and select "View Settings" to access a range of customization options, allowing you to fine-tune your notification experience.

7) **Effortlessly Clear Notifications**: When it's time to declutter your Notification Center, simply adhere to these instructions:
   a) Navigate to Notification Center.

b) Tap the "Edit" button.
c) Select "Clear" to remove all notifications, leaving your screen clean and organized.

8) **Silence All Notifications with Ease**: When you need some uninterrupted peace, enable Do Not Disturb mode. This feature ensures all notifications are silenced, allowing you to focus without interruption. Refer to our guide on turning on or scheduling a Focus on your iPad for more details.

Optimize Your App Notifications

Siri is always looking out for you! Should an application remain idle for some time, Siri might suggest turning off notifications for that app, reducing unnecessary distractions and ensuring you receive only the most relevant updates.

Stay Informed with Lock Screen Notifications

Keep recent notifications accessible even when your iPad is locked:

1. Navigate to **Settings** ⚙.
2. Subject to your device variant, select either Face ID & Passcode, Touch ID & Passcode, or Passcode.
3. Enter your passcode.
4. Toggle on Notification Center beneath "Allow Access When Locked" to ensure navigate to Notification Center from the Lock Screen.

BECOME PROFICIENT WITH YOUR IPAD'S ALERT SETUP

Assume command of your Notifications

In your iPad's Settings ⚙, you wield the power to dictate which apps can ping you, alter the alert tones, configure location-based alerts, permit or silence government notifications, and so much more.

Customize Your Notification Settings

Dive into the realm of personalized notifications! You have the liberty to tailor most notification settings for each application to your liking. You can toggle app notifications on or off, opt for audible alerts, select where and how notifications pop up when your device is active, and a myriad of other tweaks.

1) **Navigate to Settings ⚙ > Notifications.**
2) **Craft a Notification Schedule:** If you crave organization, tap on Scheduled Summary and flip the switch to activate this feature. (For more details, consult the section on scheduling a notification summary.)
3) **Tune Your Notification Previews:** Decide when you want those tantalizing notification previews to grace your screen. Tap on Show Previews, then choose among the options—Always, When Unlocked, or Never—and tap the arrow ‹ at the upper left to confirm.

These previews may encompass snippets of text from Messages and Mail or event details from Calendar. Fear not, you retain the power to override this setting on a per-app basis.

4) **Fine-Tune Your App Notifications**: Navigate to the Notification Style section, and select an application of your choice. Here, you hold the key to enabling or disabling notifications altogether. Should

163

you opt to receive notifications, take charge of their timing—whether immediate or neatly bundled in the scheduled notification summary. Additionally, toggle Time Sensitive Notifications according to your preference. For many apps, you can delve deeper by configuring notification banner styles and deciding whether to include sounds and badges.

5) **Organize Your Notifications**: Dive into Notification Grouping, where you dictate how your notifications are presented:
   a) **Automatic:** Let your iPad intelligently group notifications based on internal criteria such as topics or threads.
   b) **By App:** Consolidate all alerts from a single application into a unified bundle.
   c) **Off:** If you prefer an ungrouped approach, toggle off this feature.

To selectively mute alerts from certain application, venture to **Settings** > then press **Notifications** > press **Siri Suggestions**, and deactivate any apps you wish to silence.

When engaging the Focus feature, your iPad intelligently delays notifications to maintain your productivity flow. You can even schedule a precise time to catch up on any missed notifications with a summary. For detailed instructions, refer to the section on Scheduling a Notification Summary.

Tap into the potential of Location-Based Alerts

Harness the capabilities of location-based alerts on your iPad, where certain apps can deliver contextually relevant notifications based on your whereabouts.

Imagine receiving a gentle nudge to make that important call immediately you step into a specific location or when you're about to embark on your next journey.

Customize Your Location-Based Alerts

If these varieties of alerts don't align with your preferences, fear not, for you possess the autonomy to turn them off at your convenience.

1. Proceed to **Settings** > then hit **Privacy & Security** > select **Location Services**.
2. **Enable Location Services:** Make sure that Location Services are turned on to let apps use your device's location information.
3. **Fine-Tune App Permissions:** Navigate through the list of applications and select any that appear. Here, you have the discretion to determine should you choose to authorize the application to access your location data.

Stay Connected with Web Push Notifications

Elevate your web browsing experience by enabling standard Web Push notifications from web apps. Simply add the website icon to your Home Screen, and you'll stay effortlessly informed of any activity within the app. Once you've subscribed for push notifications within the web app, you'll receive notification alerts and badges akin to those from other Applications on Your iPad.

UNLEASH YOUR PRODUCTIVITY WITH FOCUS ON IPAD

Enter the realm of heightened concentration with the transformative Focus feature. Designed to minimize distractions and amplify your productivity, Focus offers a suite of customizable options personalized to your specific needs—be it work, personal endeavors, or restful slumber. Select from pre-defined Focus categories such as Work, Personal, or Sleep, or craft your very own Custom Focus.

Focus grants you the power to temporarily silence all notifications or selectively permit only those pertinent to your current task. Furthermore, it communicates your availability to both individuals and applications, ensuring uninterrupted focus during your hour of need.

Tailor Your Home Screen for Enhanced Focus

Immerse yourself in productivity by crafting a specialized Home Screen page dedicated to your current Focus. With iPad's intuitive suggestions, you can effortlessly curate Home Screens featuring apps and widgets aligned with your Focus, ensuring optimal efficiency during your dedicated tasks.

Maximize Focus with Quick Notifications Management

For instant tranquility, utilize the Control Center to swiftly silence all notifications. Simply access Control Center, press Focus, and enable Do Not Disturb mode.

Set Up Your Focus

When establishing a Focus, you have the liberty to handpick the apps and contacts from which you wish to receive notifications. For instance, with a Work Focus, you can pick to prioritize notifications from your colleagues and essential work-related apps.

1. **Navigate to Settings** ⚙ **> Focus.**

2. **Select Your Focus:** Choose a Focus that aligns with your current task or mindset—options include Personal, Sleep, or Work. For the selected Focus, customize the following options as desired:
   a) Notification preferences from specific apps and contacts.
   b) Personalized Home Screen Setup for your Focus.
   c) Enabling **Do Not Disturb** mode along with necessary configuration.

3. **Customize Your Notification Sources**: Define precisely which apps and contacts have the privilege of breaking through your Focus with notifications. Refer to the section titled "Silence or Allow Notifications for a Focus" for detailed instructions.
4. **Fine-Tune Your Focus Settings**: Access the Options menu to tailor your Focus experience:
   a) **Manage Silenced Notifications:** Opt to display muted alerts on the Lock Screen or redirect them to the Notification Center by toggling the "Show On Lock Screen" option.
   b) **Enhance Focus Ambiance:** Immerse yourself further by dimming the Lock Screen with the "Dim Lock Screen" feature.

c) **Streamline Your Home Screen:** Eliminate visual distractions by hiding notification badges on Home Screen apps with the "Hide Notification Badges" setting.

5. **Confirm Your Selections**: Once you've adjusted the options to your liking, tap the arrow ⟨ at the upper section of the screen to proceed.

6. **Select Your Focus Home Screen**: Handpick a dedicated Home Screen page to complement your Focus. Just select the miniature Home Screen displayed below "Customize Screens," select your preferred screen, and tap "Done." Don't forget to validate your choice by touching the checkmark icon ⟨. For further customization of your chosen Home Screen to better suit your Focus, refer to the section on "Move Apps and Widgets on the Home Screen."

7. **Sync Your Focus Across Devices:** Achieve seamless concentration throughout every Apple device you own by enabling the "Share Across Devices" feature. Ensure you're logged into all devices with a unified Apple ID to activate this functionality.

Once you've configured your Focus, you retain the flexibility to revisit Settings > Focus at your convenience. Here, you can effortlessly modify any previously selected options to better suit your evolving needs.

You have the ability to toggle a Focus on or off directly from the Control Center or even schedule automatic activation.

Align Your Sleep Focus with Your iPhone
When configuring a Sleep Focus, it adheres to the sleep schedule set on your iPhone. To manage or modify your sleep schedule, navigate to the Health application on your iPhone, press **Browse**, and select **Sleep**.

Fine-Tune Your Focus with App Filters

Elevate your Focus experience by incorporating app filters, enabling you to control the flow of information during your Focus sessions. For instance, you can specify which e-mail account or calendar to access during your Focus.

1) **Navigate to Settings** > then press **Focus.**
2) **Select Your Focus:** Choose the Focus you wish to enhance with filters.
3) **Add Filters for Added Precision**: Tap "Add Filter" located below "Focus Filters."
4) **Customize App Access:** Pick an application, then tap "Choose." From there, handpick the specific information you wish to access during your Focus:
   a) **Calendar:** Select which calendar entries you want to display during the Focus.
   b) **Mail:** Choose the mail accounts you wish to utilize during the Focus.
   c) **Messages:** Curate a list of message conversations you want to prioritize during the Focus, like those from individuals you've allowed notifications from during this period.
   d) **Safari:** Pick the Tab Group you want to access during your Focus.
5) **Seal the Deal:** After making your selections, tap "Add" to integrate the filter seamlessly into your Focus.

Craft Your Own Focus with Customization

If none of the pre-defined Focus options quite align with your task at hand, fear not—you have the freedom to create a bespoke Focus tailored to your unique needs.

1. **Navigate to Settings**  > then press **Focus.**

2. **Forge Your Path:** Tap the ✚ icon at the upper right edge, then select "Custom."

3. **Give Your Focus a Name:** Enter a descriptive name for your Focus, then tap "Return."

4. **Infuse Personality:** Select a vibrant color and an expressive icon to embody the essence of your Focus, then tap "Next."

5. **Fine-Tune Your Settings:** Refine your Focus experience by customizing any of the options outlined in step 3 of the "Set Up a Focus" instructions.

Synchronize Your Focus Across Devices
Ensure consistency throughout every Apple device you own by sharing your Focus settings effortlessly.

1. **Access Settings** > **Focus.**

2. **Activate Cross-Device Harmony:** Enable the "Share Across Devices" option to synchronize your Focus settings seamlessly throughout every Apple device you own where you're logged in with the identical Apple ID.

BOOST EFFICIENCY THROUGH PERSONALIZED ALERTS SETTINGS ON YOUR IPAD

Assume command of your notifications with the power of Focus. Whether you're in the zone for work, relaxation, or sleep, you can tailor your iPad to deliver only the notifications that are most meaningful to you.

Customize Your Focus:

1. Navigate to **Settings** > **Focus** on your iPad.
2. Select your desired Focus, such as Do Not Disturb, Personal, Sleep, or Work.

Fine-Tune Your Notifications:
1) Press "People" (or pick "Choose People").
2) Control your alert settings by:
   a) Enabling alerts from chosen contacts: Just hit 'Allow Notifications From,' and pick the individuals from your contact list.
   b) Managing incoming calls: Opt to receive Calls from specific groups or enable repeated call notifications (triggered by multiple calls within a three-minute interval).
   c) Muting particular contacts:
      (1) Assume command of your notifications by silencing specific people. Simply tap "Silence

Notifications From," then choose contacts from your address book.

(2) Optionally, enable "Allow Calls From Silenced People" for added flexibility.

(3) Note: Emergency contacts can always reach you, regardless of your Focus settings. Learn more about this feature in the section below.

Fine-Tuning App Notifications:

1) Navigate to **Settings** ⚙ > **Focus** on your iPad.
2) Select your desired Focus, such as Do Not Disturb, Work, Personal, or Sleep.
3) Tap on "Apps" (or select "Choose Apps"). Customize Your App Notifications:

   a) **Enable Chosen Applications: Select** "Allow Notifications From," then select the applications you like to receive notifications from.

   b) **Mute Certain Apps:** Press "Silence Notifications From," then choose the apps you wish to mute.

   c) **Pro Tip**: You possess the option to manage Alerts from online applications placed on your Home Screen as well. (For additional details, refer to "Receive Web Push notifications from web apps.")

Enhance Your Notification Experience: Optimize your notification flow with "Time Sensitive Notifications," ensuring that all time-sensitive alerts are delivered promptly.

Keep Others In The Loop With Your Focus Status

Stay focused and in control by sharing your Focus status with others. When you activate a Focus, it filters the notifications you receive from both people and apps. If someone outside your allowed notifications attempts to reach you, your Focus status will appear in Messages, signaling that you're currently occupied.

Here's how you can share your Focus status:

1. Navigate to **Settings > Focus > Focus Status** on your iPad.
2. Toggle on "Share Focus Status," then choose the Focus options you'd like to share your status from.

Ensure You're Always Accessible To Emergency Contacts

Even when your iPad or notifications are silenced, it's crucial to stay accessible to your emergency contacts. Here's how you can activate this feature:

1. Open the **Contacts** app on your iPad.
2. Select the desired contact, then tap "Edit."
3. Tap on "Ringtone" or "Text Tone," then activate "Emergency Bypass."

EFFORTLESSLY CONTROL YOUR FOCUS ON YOUR IPAD

Mastering your Focus settings on your iPad has never been easier. Whether you want to stay undisturbed during a crucial task or maintain a distraction-free environment for an extended period, you can switch on or schedule a Focus effortlessly.

Activate a Focus via Control Center:

1) Swipe down to launch Control Center on your iPad.
2) Locate the "Focus" button and tap on it.
3) Select the desired Focus option (e.g., Do Not Disturb).
4) Customize Your Focus Duration:

   a) To set a specific duration for your Focus, tap next to the Focus.
   b) Choose from options like "For 1 hour" or "Until I leave this location."
   c) Tap again to confirm your selection.

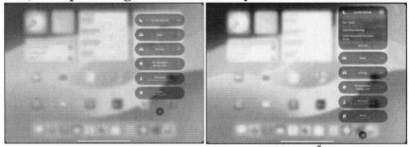

When your Focus is active, its icon, such as for Do Not Disturb, will be prominently displayed within the status bar and on the Lock Screen. Your status is also automatically communicated to your contacts via the Messages app, indicating that you've silenced notifications. However, rest assured that urgent matters can still reach you.

Pro Tip: Alternatively, you can manage your Focus settings by navigating to **Settings** > then press **Focus** and toggling the desired Focus on or off.

Effortlessly Manage Your Focus With Siri And Automated Scheduling

Tap into the potential of Siri and automated scheduling to streamline your Focus experience on your iPad. Whether you need to activate a Focus instantly or automate it to align with your daily routine, these features offer unparalleled convenience.

Activate or Deactivate a Focus with Siri:

1) Simply invoke Siri and say commands like "Turn on the Work Focus" or "Turn off the Work Focus" to toggle your Focus settings seamlessly.

Automate Focus Activation with Scheduled Settings:

1. Navigate to **Settings** > then press **Focus** on your iPad.
2. Select the desired Focus you like to schedule.
3. Enable Smart Activation by toggling the switch, then press ‹ at the upper section of the screen.
4. **Set Up Automated Scheduling:** Tap "Add Schedule" and configure the parameters based on your preferences. You can specify activation times, locations, or even trigger it based on app usage.

Note: For Sleep Focus, it adheres to the sleep schedule set in the Health application on your iPhone. To manage or modify your sleep schedule, access the Health app, tap "Browse," and then select "Sleep."

Effortlessly Disable A Focus And Remove Unneeded Ones

Once you're done with a Focus, it's easy to deactivate it and allow notifications to flow freely again. Plus, if there's

175

no further requirement for a specific Focus, you can promptly remove it from your settings.

Switch Off a Focus:

1) Choose any of these procedures:
   a) Long-press the Focus icon on your Lock Screen.
   b) Access **Control Center** and tap on "Focus."
2) Tap the active Focus to deactivate it and resume receiving notifications.

Deleting a Focus:

1. Navigate to **Settings** > then press **Focus** on your iPad.
2. Select the Focus you like to remove.
3. Scroll down to the lower part of the screen and tap "Delete Focus."

If you happen to remove a designated Focus setting, don't worry. You can easily reconfigure it anew by navigating to **Settings** > then press **Focus** and tapping on ➕ the respective option.

PERSONALIZE YOUR SHARING EXPERIENCE IN AN IPAD APP

Tailor your Share menu to your preferences by customizing the options that appear and arranging them precisely to your preference. Whether you like to streamline your workflow or prioritize your favorite sharing methods, these simple guidelines will assist you optimize your app experience.

Customize Sharing Options:

1. Open the document you wish to share within the app.

2. Tap on the "Share" icon  located within the app interface.

Access Advanced Editing:

3. Swipe left over the row of buttons, then tap "More."
4. Select "Edit" to proceed to the customization screen.

Customize Your Choices:

a) Activate an option by tapping the toggle switch adjacent to it.

b) To remove an option from view, tap the toggle switch to turn it off.

c) Include options in your Favorites by selecting the ⊕ icon.

d) Remove options from Favorites by tapping the ⊖ icon.

e) Adjust the sequence of options within Favorites by dragging the handle icon next to each option.

Wrap Up Your Customization:

5. Once you're satisfied with your adjustments, tap "Done" to save your changes.

CHAPTER 5: MASTERING TEXT INPUT ON IPAD

EFFORTLESSLY CRAFT TEXT AND GRAPHICS ON YOUR IPAD

Welcome to the realm of seamless text and graphic manipulation on your iPad. Dive into the convenience of inputting and refining text with a range of tools at your fingertips.

1. *Touch any key to initiate typing*

Entering Text with Finesse

Discover the fluidity of text entry on your iPad. Whether you're a beginner or a seasoned pro, the onscreen keyboard is your passcode to effortless expression. Simply tap any text field to summon the keyboard. Pinch to shrink it for precision typing, or embrace QuickPath for a fluid, swipe-based experience (available for select languages). Glide from one letter to the next without releasing a finger, effortlessly shaping your words.

Mastering Input Methods

Unleash your creativity with a myriad of input options. Dictation opens the door to hands-free text entry, while an external keyboard offers familiar tactile feedback. For the artist within, the Apple Pencil converts your iPad into a canvas of possibilities. Experiment, explore, and let your ideas flow freely.

Customization for Comfort

Tailor your typing experience to align with your tastes. Drag the keyboard to your desired location, granting unparalleled flexibility for one-handed typing. With this level of customization, finding your perfect setup is a breeze.

Unlock the complete capabilities Keyboard Input

Returning to the full-size keyboard is as easy as a pinch. Once expanded, unleash your typing prowess with a tap on the keys. Whether you're navigating the smaller or larger keyboard, here are some handy tricks to elevate your typing game:

1) **Seamless Shifts**: Transition between uppercase and lowercase effortlessly. Tap the shift key ⇧ or gently slide your finger from the shift key ⇧ to your desired letter, embracing the fluidity of expression.

2) **Caps Lock Convenience**: Need to emphasize a point? Double-tap the shift key ⇧ to activate Caps Lock and unleash the full force of your message.

3) **Swift Sentence Endings**: Wrap up your thoughts swiftly with a period and a space. A double-tap on the space bar concludes your sentence seamlessly, allowing for smooth transitions between ideas.

4) **Numerical Finesse**: Numbers, punctuation, and symbols are at your fingertips. Simply tap the number key 123 or the symbol key #+= to access these essential elements of communication.

5) **Spelling Support**: Mistakes happen, but correction is a breeze. Identify misspelled words with a red underline, then tap for suggested corrections. Choose the replacement or manually type the correct spelling, ensuring clarity in your message.

6) **Autocorrect Assurance**: Autocorrect offers assistance, but you're always in control. If a correction doesn't align with your intent, tap the underlined word to revert to your original spelling, maintaining the integrity of your message.

7) **Undo with Ease**: Regret a recent edit? Slide left utilizing 3 fingers or tap the "Undo" button ↩ to seamlessly revert your last action.

8) **Redo with Confidence**: Changed your mind? Slide right utilizing 3 fingers or tap the "Redo" button ↪ to confidently reinstate your last edit.

9) **Streamlined Navigation**: Need more screen space? Tap the keyboard icon ⌨ to swiftly hide the onscreen keyboard, freeing up your view for uninterrupted focus.

Immersive Keyboard Sounds

Immerse yourself in the typing experience by enabling keyboard clicks. Access **Settings** > press **Sounds**, then toggle on **Keyboard Clicks** to add auditory feedback to your typing journey.

Effortless Cursor Control

Transform your onscreen keyboard into a trackpad for precise cursor movement:

1) Glide your finger over the keyboard to reposition the cursor

1. Long-press the Space bar till the keyboard transforms light gray.
2. Navigate the cursor by dragging your finger across the keyboard.

Intuitive Text Selection

Selecting text is a breeze with the onscreen trackpad:

a) Long-press the keyboard utilizing one finger to initiate text selection.
b) Refine your selection by sliding a different finger across the keyboard.

For additional text selection techniques, explore the Select, cut, copy, and paste text feature.

Unlocking Special Characters: Adding Flair to Your Text

Enhance Your Writing with Accented Letters and Symbols. Add a touch of sophistication to your text with accented letters and unique characters. Here's how:

Intuitive Input

While typing, simply Long-press the letter, number, or symbol on the keyboard related to the character you desire. For instance, to add é to your text, Long-press the "e" key, then glide your finger to select the desired accent.

Tailored Options

Explore additional functionalities tailored to specific keyboards:

a) **Thai Keyboard**: Access native numbers by touching and holding the corresponding Arabic number.

b) **For Chinese, Japanese, or Arabic Keyboard:** Select the recommended characters or options presented above the keyboard to effortlessly integrate them into your text. Swipe left to display more options. For a comprehensive list, tap the up arrow; to revisit to the condensed view, tap the down arrow.

Seamless Text Manipulation: Mastering Text Movement

Effortlessly Rearrange Your Words

Assume command of your text with easy-to-follow steps for moving content within your favorite text editing apps:

Select and Elevate

1. Within a text editing application, select the text you intend to move.
2. Hold down on the chosen text until it rises from the page, signaling it's prepared for relocation.

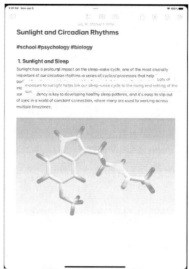

Navigate with Precision

3. With your text lifted, effortlessly drag it to your desired location within the application.

Undo with Ease

Should you have a change of heart, simply release your finger before completing the drag action, or drag the text off-screen to abandon the movement.

Customize Your Typing Experience

Enhance your typing environment by toggling special typing features on or off:

1. While typing on the onscreen keyboard, Long-press the globe 😃 or emoji 🌐 icon.
2. Select "Keyboard Settings" from the menu that appears, or navigate to **Settings** ⚙ > then press **General > Keyboard**.
3. Toggle desired typing features on or off as needed, with green indicating activation.

Effortless Text Input, Simply by Speaking

Harness the strength of speech with Dictation on your iPad, allowing you to effortlessly transform your words into text wherever typing is required. Here's strategies to optimize this feature:

Versatile Input Options

Dictation seamlessly integrates with both typing and handwriting methods, offering flexibility to align with your tastes. Whether you prefer the tactile feel of a keyboard or the precision of an Apple Pencil, Dictation adapts to your chosen input mode.

Smooth Transition

Switching between speaking and typing (or handwriting) is a breeze with Dictation. Keep the keyboard or tools palette open during Dictation, enabling you to effortlessly alternate between input methods as needed. For instance, you can pick text using touch or Apple Pencil and substitute it with your unique sound, enhancing your efficiency and productivity.

Privacy and Convenience

Speech-to-text submissions are executed directly on your device, ensuring your privacy and security. With the ability to recognize various languages and work offline, Dictation functions smoothly even without internet access. It's important to be aware, though, that dictations made into a search field might be transmitted to the search service for processing.

Usability and Factors to Keep in Mind

Though Dictation offers robust functionality, it's essential to recognize that its accessibility might differ based on your language, geographical location, or area. Additionally, data usage fees might be incurred when using Dictation, especially in Wi-Fi + Cellular models.

Enabling Dictation

1. Navigate to **Settings** > then press **General** > press **Keyboard**.
2. Toggle on "Enable Dictation." If prompted, tap "Enable Dictation" to confirm your selection.

Exploring Privacy and Security

For further information on how Apple prioritizes your privacy and allows you to control your shared information, tap "About Dictation & Privacy" located below the Dictation settings.

Initiating Voice Input:

1) Choose the text field where you want your dictated text to appear.

1) *Initiate speaking when this symbols shows up.*
2) *Hit to switch on and off Dictation*

2) Locate the microphone icon on your virtual keyboard or within any text entry field available.

3) As soon as the microphone symbol pops up above the cursor, begin speaking your desired text.

4) **Inserting Emojis and Punctuation:** To seamlessly insert emojis or punctuation marks, or perform simple formatting tasks, try these commands:

   a) **Emojis**: Simply say the name of the emoji you desire, such as "heart emoji" or "car emoji."

   b) **Punctuation**: Dictate the name of the punctuation mark, like "exclamation point."

Automated Punctuation

For recognized languages, Dictation intuitively inserts commas, full stops, and interrogation points during your dictation. If you prefer to switch off this feature, access

Settings ⚙ > press **General** > then press **Keyboard**, then toggle off Auto-Punctuation. Refer to the list below for an in-depth manual for punctuation and formatting commands compatible with Dictation.

Formatting Commands

Enhance the structure of your text by utilizing formatting commands, such as "new line" or "new paragraph," to organize your content seamlessly.

Convenient Stop Functionality

When you're finished dictating, simply tap the microphone icon 🎤 again or allow Dictation to stop automatically after 30 seconds of silence.

Multilingual Support

Enjoy the flexibility of using Dictation in multiple languages by switching keyboards accordingly.

Disabling Dictation

Should you wish to deactivate Dictation, adhere to these instructions:

1. Navigate to **Settings** ⚙ > then press **General** > **Keyboard**.
2. Toggle off "Enable Dictation" to disable the feature.

EFFORTLESSLY POSITION YOUR IPAD ONSCREEN KEYBOARD

Master the Flexibility of Your Onscreen Keyboard
Unlock the versatility of your iPad's onscreen keyboard effortlessly. Based on the specific version of your iPad,

you have the ability to customize your typing experience—whether you prefer a floating, movable keyboard, a split layout at the lower part of your screen, or an undocked version perfectly centered.

Opt for a Floating Keyboard

Navigate to your preferred typing spot with ease by utilizing the floating keyboard feature:

1. Simply tap into any text field to summon the onscreen keyboard.

2. Press and hold the keyboard icon ⌨, then glide your finger to choose the 'Floating' option, releasing upon indication. Observe the emergence of a compact keyboard, prepared to follow you anywhere on your display.

3. Engage with your content effortlessly—type by tapping keys or seamlessly slide from one letter to the next without lifting a finger (note: this feature may not be available for all languages).

4. Must return to the full-width keyboard? No problem. Pinch the floating version open, and voila!

Unlock the Split Keyboard Feature

Tailor Your Typing Experience with Split Keyboard
Elevate your typing game by activating the Split Keyboard feature, available on compatible iPad models. Whether you're multitasking, enhancing ergonomics, or simply seeking a fresh approach to typing, splitting your keyboard is the way to go.

Activate Split Keyboard

Choose your preferred method to enable the Split Keyboard setting:

1) Navigate to **Settings** ⚙ > then press **General** > **Keyboard**, and toggle Split Keyboard on or off.
2) Alternatively, access Keyboard Settings by touching and holding 😊 or 🌐 then pick Split Keyboard.

Master Split Keyboard Functionality

Once Split Keyboard is enabled, effortlessly manipulate your keyboard layout:

1) Tap into any text field to summon the onscreen keyboard.
2) To split the keyboard, Long-press the keyboard icon ⌨, then glide your finger to select "Split" and release.
3) Need to reunite your keyboard? No sweat. Long-press the keyboard icon ⌨ again, glide your finger to select "Merge," and release.

Liberate Your Keyboard: Undock with Ease

Experience Unrestricted Typing with Undocked Keyboard

Unleash the complete capabilities your iPad's keyboard by undocking it from its default position. With Split Keyboard activated in your settings, you have the ability to elevate your typing experience to new heights.

Seamlessly Undock Your Keyboard

Proceed with the following straightforward instructions to undock your keyboard:

1) Initiate a text field to summon the onscreen keyboard.

2) Long-press the keyboard icon⌨, then glide your finger to select "Undock" before releasing. Witness as your keyboard gracefully ascends from the bottom of your screen.

3) Now, revel in the freedom to type with your keyboard in this elevated position.

Restore to Default Position

When you're ready to return your undocked keyboard to its original spot, adhere to these instructions:

1. Long-press the keyboard icon⌨ once more.
2. Glide your finger to select "Dock," then release. Watch as your keyboard seamlessly returns to its familiar position near the screen's bottom.

EFFORTLESSLY MANIPULATE TEXT ON YOUR IPAD

Perfect the skill of Selecting, Cutting, Copying, and Pasting

Empower yourself with the ability to edit text seamlessly within various Applications on Your iPad. With the onscreen keyboard as your trusty tool, you'll navigate the world of text editing with finesse and precision.

Select and Refine Your Text

Uncover multiple methods to select text effortlessly:

1. **Select a Word:** Simply double-tap utilizing one finger to highlight a single word.
2. **Select a Paragraph:** Elevate your selection skills by triple-tapping utilizing one finger to encompass an entire paragraph.
3. **Select a Block of Text:** Take control of larger sections by double-tapping and holding the first word, then smoothly dragging to encompass the entire block.

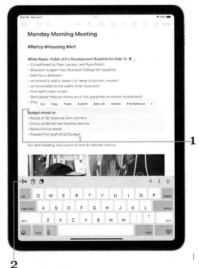

1) *Shift the anchor points to modify the selection.*
2) *Press to slice, duplicate, and insert the chosen text.*

Refine Your Selection with Ease

Once your desired text is selected, dive into the domain of editing with these intuitive gestures:

1. **Cut:** Trim your selection with precision by tapping "Cut" or employing a quick pinch gesture with three fingers, twice.
2. **Copy:** Duplicate your selection effortlessly with a tap of "Copy" or a simple pinch gesture with three fingers.
3. **Paste:** Seamlessly integrate copied text into your desired location by tapping "Paste" or executing a gentle pinch gesture with three fingers, in the opposite direction.
4. **Replace:** Explore suggested replacement text or let Siri offer alternative options for your selection.
5. **Format:** Fine-tune the appearance of your selected text with various formatting options.
6. **Explore Further** ▶ : Delve into additional editing options to unlock even more potential.

Pro Tip: Need to relocate text without cutting or copying? Simply Long-press the selected text until it lifts up, then effortlessly drag it to its new destination.

Position Your Insertion Point

1) **Choose Your Spot:** Navigate to the exact location where you wish to insert text by employing any of these procedures:
   a) Just select the desired insertion point within your document.
   b) For precise positioning, touch and hold to enlarge the text, then effortlessly shift the cursor by moving it to your desired location.

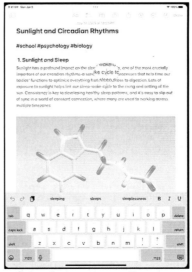

2) **Effortless Navigation:** In longer documents, streamline your navigation process by touching and holding the right-edge of the document. Then, smoothly drag the scroller to locate the specific section where you like to make revisions.

Add Your Text

3. **Type Away:** Once your insertion point is set, unleash your creativity by typing or pasting the text you wish to add. Whether it's a single word, a paragraph, or a snippet of code, the process remains intuitive and seamless.

Bonus Tip: Tap into the potential of Universal Clipboard to seamlessly cut or copy content from one Apple device and paste it onto another. Experience unparalleled continuity in your workflow as you effortlessly transition between devices.

STREAMLINE YOUR WRITING WITH PREDICTIVE TEXT

Effortless Typing at Your Fingertips

Unlock the power of predictive text on your iPad and revolutionize the way you compose messages, emails, notes, and more. With predictive text, crafting entire sentences becomes a breeze, requiring only a handful of touches to convey your thoughts effectively.

Seamless Integration of Suggestions

1. **Dynamic Suggestions:** As you type on the iPad keyboard, predictive text springs into action, presenting you with a plethora of choices for words, emojis, and even information you're likely to type next (note: availability varies by language).
2. **Smart Contextual Predictions:** In applications like Messages, predictive text anticipates your needs based on context. For instance:
    a) Begin typing "I'm at," and watch as your current location conveniently appears as an option.
    b) Similarly, inputting "My number is" prompts your phone number to emerge as a suggested completion.

Harnessing Inline Predictions

3. **Seamless Integration:** Inline predictions seamlessly integrate into your typing flow, appearing in gray text as you compose. Simply Hit the Space bar to confirm the suggested word or phrase, or keep typing to dismiss it.
4. **Flexible Corrections:** you confirm the suggested text, proceed to have a change of heart, fear not.

   Easily revert by tapping the backspace key ⌫, followed by the term you were actively composing.

Note: While inline predictive text enhances your typing experience, please be aware that support may vary depending on your language.

Effortlessly Apply Predictive Text

Enhance Your Typing Efficiency

Leverage the power of predictive text on your iPad to streamline your typing experience like never before. As you type, watch as suggested words, emojis, and even relevant information gracefully appear above your onscreen keyboard, ready to be applied through a straightforward press.

Applying Suggestions with Ease

1. **Seamless Integration:** Stay in the flow of your writing as predictive text suggestions seamlessly appear above your onscreen keyboard. Simply tap on a suggestion to apply it to your text.

1) *Predictive keyboard; press a hint to adopt*

2. **Automatic Spacing:** Upon accepting a suggested word, rest assured that a space will automatically be entered after the suggestion. However, be mindful that if you input punctuation such as a comma or period, the preceding space will be deleted automatically.

Rejecting Suggestions

a) Should you wish to bypass the suggestions provided, either touch your original word (displayed within quotation marks) or continue typing to proceed with your intended text.

Disabling Predictive Text

1) If predictive text isn't your cup of tea, fear not. You can decide to switch it off:

   a) For onscreen keyboards: Long-press the ☺ or ⊕, then navigate to Keyboard Settings and toggle off Predictive.

   b) Utilizing an external keyboard: Head to **Settings** ◉ > then press **General** > press **Keyboard**, then switch off Predictive.

Fine-Tuning Corrections

Even with predictive text turned off, iPad may still offer adjustments for typographical errors. To confirm an edit, press the spacebar, add punctuation, or hit **Return**. To dismiss an edit, select the 'x'. If you consistently reject a particular suggestion, iPad learns to stop suggesting it.

Keep in mind: Switching off the Predictive option will deactivate both the predictive text feature and the inline suggestions.

EFFORTLESSLY SAVE KEYSTROKES UTILIZING TEXT REPLACEMENTS

Enhance Your Typing Efficiency

Maximize your productivity on iPad by setting up text replacements, allowing you to enter commonly used words or phrases with just a few keystrokes. Streamline your communication and workflow with this handy feature, ensuring that frequently typed expressions are at your fingertips whenever you need them.

Setting Up Text Replacements

1) **Initiate Setup:**

   a) For onscreen keyboards: Long-press the 😊 or 🌐, then navigate to Keyboard Settings and tap Text Replacement.

   b) Utilizing an external keyboard: Navigate to **Settings** ⚙ >then press **General** > **Keyboard**, then tap **Text Replacement**.

2) **Add a New Replacement:**

   a) Tap the ➕ icon located at the upper right-edge of the screen.

   b) Enter the desired phrase within the Phrase field, along with the corresponding text shortcut you wish to utilize for it in the Shortcut box.

Optimizing for Custom Entries

1) If you have a specific word or phrase that you frequently use and don't want it to be corrected:

   a) Navigate to **Settings** ⚙ > then press **General** > **Keyboard**, then tap **Text Replacement**.

b) Tap the ╋ icon at the upper right edge.
c) Type your selected word or expression into the designated Phrase area, leaving the Shortcut field blank.

Enhance Typing Efficiency with Word and Input Pairs

Seamless Integration for Chinese and Japanese Keyboards

Elevate your typing experience on iPad with the ability to create text replacements for word and input pairs, particularly when using Chinese or Japanese keyboards. By establishing these replacements, you can effortlessly substitute specific words or inputs for designated shortcuts, thereby enhancing your productivity and communication in languages such as Simplified Chinese, Traditional Chinese, and Japanese.

Supported Shortcuts

1) For Simplified Chinese keyboards: Utilize Pinyin input.
2) For Traditional Chinese keyboards: Access shortcuts for both Pinyin and Zhuyin inputs.
3) For Japanese keyboards: Leverage shortcuts for Romaji and Kana inputs.

Sync Across Devices with iCloud

1) Keep your personal dictionary synchronized across all your gadgets using iCloud:

   a) Access **Settings** ⚙ > press **[your name]** > then press **iCloud**.
   b) Activate iCloud Drive to ensure seamless integration across your Apple ecosystem.

Resetting Your Personal Dictionary

1) Should the need arise to reset your personal dictionary to its default state:

   a) Navigate to **Settings** > then press **General** > press **Transfer or Reset iPad** > **Reset**.

   b) Tap "Reset Keyboard Dictionary" and confirm the action.

2) Upon resetting, all custom words and shortcuts will be erased, reverting the keyboard dictionary to its default configuration.

UNLOCK MULTILINGUAL TYPING: MASTER ADDING AND CHANGING KEYBOARDS ON YOUR IPAD

Effortlessly Type in Multiple Languages and Customize Your Keyboard Layout

Unlocking the complete capabilities OF your iPad's keyboard is simpler than you might think. Whether you're a seasoned linguist, a digital nomad, or simply seeking to broaden your linguistic horizons, becoming proficient in adding and changing keyboards opens an array of potential opportunities. Gone are the days of fumbling with language settings or struggling to switch between keyboards. Embrace the ease of learning and the convenience of seamless multilingual typing.

ADDING OR SWITCHING KEYBOARDS: A STEP-BY-STEP GUIDE

Tap into the capabilities of your iPad's versatility by adding keyboards for writing or dictation in various languages. Plus, customize the layout of your on-screen or external keyboard to align with your tastes. Here's how:

1) Navigate to **Settings** > then press **General** > select **Keyboard**.
2) Click on 'Keyboards', then follow these simple steps:
   a) **To add a Keyboard:** Hit 'Add New Keyboard' and choose your preferred keyboard from the list. Repeat this procedure to seamlessly add multiple keyboards.
   b) **Removing and Reordering Keyboards: Simplifying Your Selection:** Removing a keyboard you no longer require is as simple as a few taps. Adhere to these instructions:
      i). Tap **Edit**.
      ii). Locate the keyboard you wish to remove and tap the minus sign next to it.
      iii). Confirm the deletion by tapping **Delete**, then tap **Done** to complete the process.
   c) To reorder your keyboard list for optimal accessibility:
      i). Tap **Edit**.
      ii). Drag the handles next to a keyboard to rearrange its position in the list.
      iii). Tap **Done** to save your changes.

By effortlessly managing your keyboard list, you ensure that your most frequently utilized languages are readily accessible, enhancing your typing experience.

Preferred Language Order: Tailoring Your Linguistic Landscape

When adding a keyboard for a different language, it automatically joins the Preferred Language Order list. Customize this list to your preference:

1. Access **Settings** > then press **General** > **Language & Region**.
2. View and modify the Preferred Language Order list according to your linguistic priorities.

By curating this list, you dictate how apps and websites display text, ensuring a seamless and personalized user experience.

SEAMLESS KEYBOARD SWITCHING: ENHANCING ACCESSIBILITY

Switching between keyboards is a breeze on your iPad:

1) On the on-screen keyboard, Long-press the globe icon ⊕ or the emoji icon ☺, then select the desired keyboard from the list.

2) Alternatively, tap the globe icon ⊕ or the emoji icon ☺ repeatedly to cycle through enabled keyboards.

3) **External Keyboard Shortcuts**: Effortlessly cycle between emoji, English, and additional keyboards added for other languages using your external keyboard:

   a) Hold down the Control key and then hit the Space bar to toggle between available keyboards. With the Magic Keyboard for iPad   and Smart Keyboard, streamline your workflow even further.

   b) Utilize the globe icon ⊕ key to swiftly switch from one keyboard to another.

CUSTOMIZING KEYBOARD LAYOUTS: TAILORING YOUR TYPING EXPERIENCE

Explore alternative keyboard layouts that better suit your preferences:

1. Navigate to **Settings** > then press **General > Keyboard > Keyboards**.
2. Select a language displayed at the screen's upper section, then pick a different layout from the options provided.

UNLOCK THE FUN: MASTERING EMOJI AND STICKERS ON YOUR IPAD KEYBOARD

Enhance Your Expression with Ease

Expressing yourself just got more colorful! Instead of sticking to plain text, immerse yourself in a realm of emoji and stickers to truly bring your messages and documents to life.

STEP INTO THE EMOJI UNIVERSE

1. Open any text field, then effortlessly switch to the emoji keyboard by tapping the globe or smiley icon.

2. Explore a plethora of options by sliding left or right, or simply tap a category symbol below to instantly navigate.

3. Select the perfect emoji to inject personality into your text through a straightforward press.

Discover Variations

Uncover the full spectrum of expression by holding down an emoji. Delight in exploring different skin tones and variations, then release to select your favorite.

Seamless Integration

Transition back to the regular keyboard with ease by tapping ABC, ensuring effortless toggling between text and visuals.

Bonus Tip

Let the keyboard do the work for you! As you type, suggested emoji will appear above the keyboard. Simply tap to seamlessly replace text with vibrant visuals.

ELEVATE YOUR VISUALS: ELEVATING MESSAGES AND DOCUMENTS WITH STICKERS

Unlock a World of Creativity: Personalize Your Communication with Stickers

Bring Your Messages to Life with Stickers

Looking to add flair to your messages and documents? Look no further than stickers! Transform ordinary text into eye-catching visuals that truly stand out.

Easy Access, Infinite Possibilities

1. Access stickers effortlessly by tapping the globe ⊕ or smiley ☺ icon to rotate to the emoji keyboard.
2. Explore your sticker collection by tapping the sticker icon ◔, where you'll find all your stickers neatly organized.

Discover Your Favorites

Your most-used stickers are just a tap away in the Frequently Used section, ensuring quick access to your preferred visuals.

Simply tap a sticker to instantly incorporate it into your message or document. For even more convenience, drag a sticker directly from the menu to your desired location.

Unleash Your Creativity

Explore a world of possibilities by downloading sticker packs from the Application Store or crafting your own personalized stickers within the Messages or Photos app.

CAPTURING MEMORIES: MASTERING SCREENSHOTTING ON YOUR IPAD

Unlock the power to preserve and share your iPad screen effortlessly.

CAPTURING THE MOMENT WITH FACE ID ENABLED IPADS

1) Simply, tap and let go of the top button and any volume button simultaneously.
   a) Witness a thumbnail swiftly materialize in the lower-left corner.
2) Tap the thumbnail to revel in your screenshot or swipe left to bid it adieu.

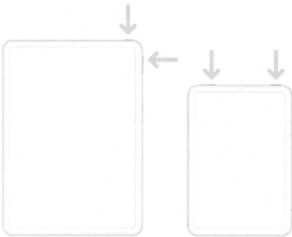

Rest assured, all your screenshots are securely tucked away in your photo library within the Photos app . To peruse them collectively, navigate to Photos, then tap on Screenshots beneath Media Types in the Photos sidebar.

CAPTURING SCREENSHOTS WITH TOUCH ID ENABLED IPADS

1) With nimble fingers, swiftly tap and let go of the top and the Home buttons in unison.

a) Behold the emergence of a thumbnail in the lower-left edge.

2) **Exploring Your Screenshots**
   a) Tap on the thumbnail to revel in your screenshot's glory or swipe left to bid it adieu.

   b) Rest assured, your precious snapshots are instantly archived in your Photos app collection.

3) **Organizing Your Collection**
   a) Seamlessly locate all your screenshots by opening Photos and tapping on Screenshots below Media Types in the Photos sidebar.

CAPTURING THE WHOLE PICTURE: FULL-PAGE SCREENSHOTS

Embrace the ability to capture extensive content with ease, such as entire webpages in Safari.

1) **Initiating the Capture**
   a) On iPads equipped with Face ID: Swiftly tap and let go of the top button and any volume button simultaneously.

b) On iPads featuring a Home button: Quickly tap and let go of the top and the Home buttons concurrently.

2) **Exploring Your Masterpiece**
   a) Tap on the screenshot thumbnail nestled in the lower-left corner to unveil the entirety of your captured content.

3) **Unleash Full Potential with Full-Page Screenshots**
   a) Select "Full Page" and tap "Done." Then, choose any one of these:
      i) "Save to Photos": Store your screenshot securely in your Photos library.
      ii) "Save PDF to Files": Opt for a specific location within the Files app to preserve your screenshot.

VENTURING INTO SCREEN RECORDING ON IPAD

Dive into the domain of screen recording to capture dynamic moments on your iPad.

1. **Prepare for Recording**: Navigate to **Settings** > then press **Control Center**, then toggle on Screen Recording.

2. **Initiate Recording**: Access Control Center by swiping down from the screen's top right, press the Screen Recording icon , then patiently await the 3-second countdown.

3. **Halt the Recording**: Cease recording by tapping the red circle ⬛ atop the screen, then confirm.

Rest assured, your screen recordings find a safe haven in your photo library within the Photos app 🌸. Easily locate them by accessing Photos and tapping on Screen Recordings under Media Types in the Photos sidebar.

Please Note: While screen recordings may encompass both audio and video elements, certain apps may restrict recording capabilities for one or the other. Additionally, simultaneous screen mirroring and screen recording are not supported.

UNLEASH YOUR CREATIVITY: MASTERING MARKUP TOOLS ON IPAD

Unlock the power to write and draw directly within your documents with Markup tools on iPad. Whether you're composing emails, jotting down notes, or enhancing your photos, Markup makes it effortless to add your personal touch.

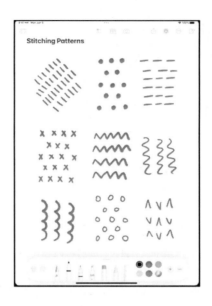

Accessing the Markup Toolbar

To harness the complete capabilities Markup tools, simply Adhere to these instructions to access the Markup toolbar in supported apps like Mail, Notes, Messages, and Photos:

1) Press the Markup icon Ⓐ or select Markup from the options.

2) Customize your toolbar placement: Drag it towards any side of the display for convenience. (Simply drag from the center edge closest to the screen's center.)

3) Streamline your workflow: Enable Auto-minimize to automatically hide the toolbar while drawing or typing. Easily access the full toolbar by tapping its minimized version.

4) Simplify as needed: Hide the toolbar altogether with a tap on the Ⓐ or Done button.

Express Yourself: Writing and Drawing

1) In any supported app, initiate Markup by tapping the designated icon Ⓐ.

2) **Choose Your Tool**
   a) Press the marker, pen, or pencil tool from the Markup toolbar.
   b) Express yourself freely by writing or drawing using your fingertip or an Apple Pencil (compatible with select iPad versions).

Customize Your Creations

While writing or drawing, personalize your creations with the following options:

a) **Adjust Line Weight:** Tap the selected drawing tool, then pick your preferred line weight.

b) **Fine-Tune Opacity:** Modify the opacity by dragging the slider to your desired level.

c) **Play with Colors:** Select a color from the color picker and further refine it by tapping Grid, Spectrum, or Sliders.

d) **Undo Mistakes:** Fear not mistakes—simply tap the Undo button ↺ to correct any mishaps.

Enhance Precision with Ruler Tool

1) **Draw Straight Lines:** Activate the ruler tool, then draw along its edge for precision.

2) **Rotate and Move with Ease:**
   a) To change the ruler's angle, touch and hold it with two fingers, then rotate.
   b) For seamless movement without altering the angle, drag the ruler with one finger.

3) **Toggle Ruler Visibility:** Easily hide or reveal the ruler by tapping the ruler tool in the toolbar.

4) To bid farewell to the Markup toolbar, simply tap the or Done button.

In apps like Notes, elevate your efficiency to new heights with Apple Pencil:

a) Write utilizing your Apple Pencil and witness your handwriting seamlessly convert to typed text instantly. Explore further with Select and edit drawings and handwriting options.

Pro Tip: Maximize efficiency with these handy tricks:

b) Utilize your Apple Pencil to swiftly take a screenshot by sliding upward starting at the bottom-left corner of the screen. Immediately begin marking it up to enhance your workflow. Don't have an Apple Pencil? No problem! Capture a screenshot and press the thumbnail that briefly appears in the lower-left corner to start editing.

Refine Your Creations: Moving and Editing Handwritten Text or Drawings

1) Activate the Lasso tool (located between the eraser and ruler) within the Markup toolbox.
2) Pick the content you wish to modify:
   a) Double-tap to pick a word or drawn object.
   b) Tap thrice to highlight a sentence.
3) Picking Paragraphs or Text Blocks:
   a) Long-press the initial word, then drag to the last word to encompass the entire paragraph or text block. For precise selection, drag slowly.

In the Notes application, Markup distinguishes between handwritten text and drawn objects, allowing separate selection:

a) **Selecting Handwritten Text Alone:** For handwritten text selection, simply drag over it. To include drawings, encompass them within your selection as well.

b) **Selecting Multiple Drawn Objects:** With the Lasso tool activated, use your Apple Pencil or finger to draw around the objects. Once selected, tap the grouped selection to proceed.

Quick Note: If the Markup toolbar isn't visible, Press the Markup icon Ⓐ to reveal it. Should the toolbar be collapsed, press its minimized version for full access.

Refining Your Revisions

1) After picking your desired content, tap it, then explore these editing options:

   a) **Cut, Copy, Delete, or Duplicate:** Tap the corresponding action to refine your content effortlessly.

   b) **Move Content:** Long-press the content until it lifts, then seamlessly relocate it to a new spot on your document.

Top Tip: Customize your handwritten text and drawings effortlessly:

a) Alter their color by tapping a color within the Markup toolbar.

b) Easily reposition them by dragging to a new location.

In iPad apps supporting Markup, enjoy the convenience of converting handwritten text to typed text instantly:

c) Explore further with Scribble on iPad for seamless text entry.

For additional ways to fine-tune your handwriting or drawings in Notes:

d) Refer to the Draw or Write in Notes on iPad guide for comprehensive editing options.

Rectify Mistakes Effortlessly

If the Markup toolbar isn't visible, Press the Markup icon Ⓐ to access it. If minimized, tap its compact version for full functionality.

1) **Erase Missteps:** Select the eraser tool from the Markup toolbar, then execute any one of these actions:

   a) **Pixel Eraser:** Eradicate individual pixels by scrubbing over the mistake with your Apple Pencil or finger.

   b) **Object Eraser:** Eliminate entire objects by touching them with your Apple Pencil or finger.

   c) **Toggle Between Erasers:** Switch seamlessly between Pixel and Object Erasers by tapping the eraser tool and making your selection.

PERFECT THE SKILL OF MARKING UP DOCUMENTS ON YOUR IPAD

Unlocking Creativity and Precision

Discover the seamless world of Markup tools on your iPad, enabling you to seamlessly enhance your images and documents with text, shapes, signatures, stickers, and more.

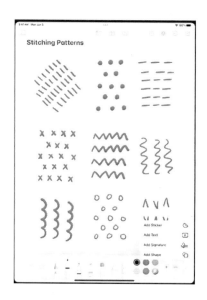

<u>Adding Text Made Easy</u>

1. Launch a supported application and press the Markup icon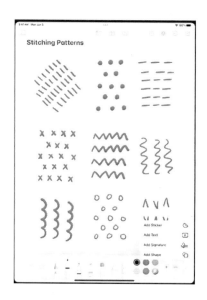.
2. Access the Markup toolbar and select "Add Text."
3. Simply tap within the document to create a text box, then input your desired text using the keyboard.
4. Customize your text's appearance by adjusting font, size, justification, style, or color using the intuitive options at the lower edge of the Markup toolbar.
5. Once satisfied, tap outside the text box to finalize your addition.
6. Conclude by tapping the Markup icon again or simply tap "Done" to dismiss the Markup toolbox.

For further modifications such as cutting, copying, duplicating, sharing, or deleting a text box, simply tap the desired text box, tap the additional options icon beside it, and select your preferred action.

Easily Insert And Modify Text, Shapes, And More

Effortless Customization at Your Fingertips

In apps like Notes, adding typed text is a breeze. You can seamlessly integrate text directly into your notes without navigating through the Markup toolbar.

Adding Typed Text

1) If the Markup toolbar is open, simply close it by tapping the designated icon Ⓐ.
2) Adhere to these instructions:
   a) Tap within the note.
   b) Utilize the onscreen or wireless keyboard to type your text. For detailed guidance, refer to "Create and Format Notes on iPad."
   c) Alternatively, employ the Apple Pencil and Scribble feature for text input. For further insight, explore "Enter Text with Scribble on iPad."

Introducing Shapes

1) Within a supported app, access the Markup Ⓐ feature.
2) Navigate to the Markup toolbar and select "Add Shape."
3) Choose your desired shape, then proceed with the following actions:
   a) Move the shape effortlessly by dragging it to your preferred location.
   b) Resize the shape by dragging any dot along its outline.
   c) Fine-tune the shape's appearance by adjusting border color, border width, fill color, and opacity through the options available in the Markup toolbox.

Fine-Tuning Shapes

a) To alter the shape's direction or dimensions, effortlessly maneuver any green dot along its outline.

b) For additional alterations such as cut, copy, duplicate, share, or delete, tap the specified icon ⊙ adjacent to the shape, then choose your intended operation.

Once content with your modifications, merely touch the screen to validate.

Closing the Markup Session

To conclude your Markup session, tap either the Markup icon ⓐ or the "Done" button to dismiss the Markup toolbox.

Pro Tip: Utilize the pinch gesture to zoom in on the document for precise adjustments to shapes. When zoomed in, seamlessly pan across the document by dragging two fingers. To turn back to the original view, simply pinch the screen closed.

Drawing Perfect Shapes

Unleash your creativity with Markup's ability to effortlessly draw geometrically perfect shapes such as lines, arcs, and more, ideal for diagrams and sketches.

1. Launch a supported app and access the Markup ⓐ feature.

2. Within the Markup toolbar, select the desired drawing tool—pen, marker, or pencil—to begin your artistic journey.

3. Utilizing your Apple Pencil or finger (on compatible iPad models), draw the shape in one fluid stroke.

4. Pause, and witness the magic as a flawless rendition of the shape seamlessly replaces your drawing. If you prefer to retain the freehand charm, simply hit the indicated icon ↶.

Variety at Your Disposal
Explore an array of shapes at your fingertips, including straight lines, arrows, arcs, continuous lines with 90-degree turns, squares, circles, rectangles, triangles, pentagons, chat bubbles, hearts, stars, and clouds.

Adding Your Signature

1) Launch a supported app and access the Markup Ⓐ feature.
2) Within the Markup toolbar, select "Add Signature."
3) Utilize your Apple Pencil or finger to effortlessly sign your name.
4) To start afresh, simply tap "Clear" and sign your name again.
5) Once done, tap "Done" to finalize your signature placement.

Fine-Tuning Your Signature
a) Move your signature with ease by dragging it to your preferred location.
b) Adjust the signature's size by dragging any dot along the outline.
c) Customize the line weight or color of your signature through options available in the Markup toolbox.
d) For additional actions such as cutting, copying, duplicating, sharing, or deletion, Hit the indicated

icon⊙ next to the signature, then select your desired option.

e) Once you've perfected the placement of your signature, simply tap outside the text box to confirm its position.

Managing Signatures

iPad simplifies the process of managing signatures, enabling you to seamlessly add or delete them as needed. Create multiple signatures, including variations like nicknames or initials, and maintain control over your signature collection.

Adding or Deleting Signatures

1. Launch a supported app and access the Markup Ⓐ feature.
2. Within the Markup toolbar, select "Add Signature."
3. Tap "Add or Remove Signature," then hit the designated icon ✛ to generate a fresh signature.
4. Proceed by tapping the arrow next to "New Signature" and selecting the desired type, such as given name, nickname, or initials.
5. Utilize your Apple Pencil or finger to craft your signature, then tap "Done."

Deleting Signatures
To remove a signature, adhere to these instructions:
1. Tap the "Add Signature" icon.
2. Select "Add or Remove Signature."
3. Hit the indicated icon ⊖ next to any signatures you wish to delete.

Spice Up Your Documents With Stylish Stickers

Injecting Fun and Personality

Refine your documents and images with the charm of stickers using Markup tools. Explore a world of creativity and expression with this delightful feature.

Adding Stickers

1. Launch a supported app and access the Markup Ⓐ feature.
2. Within the Markup toolbar, select "Add Sticker."
3. Browse through your sticker collection and touch the desired sticker, then effortlessly drag it onto your document or photo.

Fine-Tuning Stickers

4. To adjust the angle of the sticker, rotate a second finger around it before lifting your finger.
5. Touch and drag a dot around the outline of the sticker to resize it according to your preference.

Expand Your Collection

Download additional sticker packs from the Application Store to further enrich your creative arsenal. Alternatively, create personalized stickers within the Messages app or by extracting subjects from photos and Live Photos.

Crafting Custom Image Descriptions

Enrich your images with descriptive context using Markup tools, particularly beneficial for accessibility purposes in supported applications like Photos.

1. Access a supported app and activate the Markup Ⓐ feature.
2. Within the Markup toolbar, select "Description."

3. Input your custom description and tap "Done" to finalize.

MASTER FORM FILLING AND SIGNING ON YOUR IPAD

Effortlessly Manage Documents and Forms

Unlock the convenience of filling out forms and signing documents seamlessly on your iPad. Empower yourself to efficiently handle paperwork, add your signature, and effortlessly share completed documents with others. Additionally, leverage the power of AutoFill to expedite the form-filling process by utilizing information stored in your Contacts application.

STREAMLINED FORM FILLING AND SIGNATURE ADDITION

1) Begin by touching the file to open the document.
2) If instructed, access the document through the Files application, then proceed by tapping "Save."
3) Hit the indicated icon, then select a blank field within the document to input text utilizing the onscreen keyboard.
4) To fill out additional fields, simply tap on each one and enter the required information.
5) Widen your choices by selecting the indicated icon, then consider the subsequent steps:
   a) **For text insertion:** Choose 'Insert Text Form Box,' position the text box where needed on the form, and begin typing with the virtual keyboard.

b) **To sign the document:** Opt for 'Insert Signature,' then use your finger or an Apple Pencil to sign. After signing, press 'Complete' and smoothly move your signature to the preferred spot in the document.

6) Upon completion, hit the indicated icon to share the document via Mail, Messages, or AirDrop.

7) Finally, tap "Done" to neatly close the document and conclude the process.

SIMPLIFY FORM FILLING WITH AUTOFILL

Harness the convenience of AutoFill to swiftly enter your personal details into supported forms and documents. As long as you've completed your My Card in the Contacts application , you can expedite the form-filling process effortlessly.

1. Begin by touching the file to open the document.

2. Hit the indicated icon , then select a blank field within the document.

3. Choose an option from your saved contact information to automatically populate the field. Alternatively, select "Choose other" to utilize AutoFill for another person's details from your contact list, such as a family member or caregiver.

4. Make any necessary changes by tapping on a field to pick it, then tapping again to edit using the onscreen keyboard.

5. Tap "Done" to seamlessly close the document and complete the process.

UNLEASH THE POWER OF LIVE TEXT ON YOUR IPAD UNLOCKING TEXT INTERACTION IN PHOTOS AND VIDEOS

When you delve into your photo gallery within the Photos app, something remarkable awaits. Live Text, with its intuitive capabilities, identifies text and data nestled within your images, granting you a myriad of possibilities for engagement. Seamlessly select, copy, share, or translate text, or effortlessly execute quick actions such as initiating a call, exploring a website, or even converting currencies.

Live Text isn't confined solely to the Photos app ; its reach extends across Safari, Camera, Quick Look, and beyond, ensuring its utility pervades your iPad experience.

ENLARGE, ENGAGE, CONVERT, AND EXAMINE TEXT WITHIN YOUR VISUALS

Before embarking on your Live Text journey, ensure it's primed for action across all supported languages:

1. Navigate to **Settings** > press **General** > **Language & Region**.
2. Activate Live Text (the vibrant green signifies readiness).

COMMAND THE POWER OF TEXT IN YOUR VISUAL MEDIA

1) Unveil a photo or pause a video harboring textual elements.

2) Tap on the icon, then Long-press the desired text to unleash an array of potential opportunities.

3) Once you've identified the text within your visual content, take charge using the grab points for pinpoint accuracy. With a simple touch, you can perform a variety of actions to match your necessities:

   a) **Copy Text**: Extract text for seamless integration into apps like Notes or Messages.

   b) **Select All**: Effortlessly capture all text within the frame.

   c) **Look Up**: Uncover personalized web suggestions at your fingertips.

   d) **Translate**: Bridge language barriers with instant text translation.

   e) **Search the Web**: Delve deeper into selected text with a swift web search.

   f) **Share**: Spread the textual wealth via AirDrop, Messages, Mail, or other available avenues.

4) Touch ⬚ to revert back to the photograph or video.

UNLOCK QUICK ACTIONS FOR EFFORTLESS TASK EXECUTION

Navigate tasks within your visual content effortlessly with quick actions conveniently located at your screen's bottom. Depending on the nature of your photo or video, a simple tap can initiate actions such as making a call, obtaining directions, translating languages, converting currencies, and much more.

1. Launch the Photos app and access a picture or halt a clip containing text.

2. Tap on the designated icon ⬚ to explore an array of potential opportunities.

3. Effortlessly execute tasks within your visual content by tapping into the array of quick actions conveniently situated at your screen's bottom. Move around with simplicity and accuracy, then just touch ⬚

Smooth Transition Back to Your Visual Content
Once you've completed your task, smoothly switch back to your image or video by touching
Note: The availability of Live Text may vary based on your region or language.

EXPLORE THE WORLD AROUND YOU WITH VISUAL LOOK UP ON IPAD

Unveil the hidden treasures within your photographs and videos with Visual Look Up, your gateway to discovering

225

popular landmarks, statues, artwork, flora, fauna, and more, all seamlessly integrated into the Photos application.

Visual Look Up even extends its gaze to culinary delights, identifying food within your frames and suggesting delectable recipes for your culinary adventures.

1)   *Visual Look Up is accessible*

1. Dive into a full-screen photo or halt a clip at any frame. Should the Info button feature star symbols like ⓘ or 🐾 , Visual Look Up stands ready.

2. Activate the starred Information button, then hit Look Up atop the picture information to unveil the wonders of Visual Look Up.

3. Conclude your exploration of Visual Look Up by tapping anywhere outside the results box, effortlessly closing it. Then, simply tap ✕ to bid farewell to the photo or video info box, returning you to your captivating visual experience.

Note: Visual Look Up may not be accessible in every regions or languages.

ELEVATE YOUR SUBJECT FROM THE BACKGROUND ON IPAD

In the immersive realm of the Photos application , you hold the power to extract the essence of a picture or video frame, isolating its subject from its background with precision. Once liberated, your subject awaits myriad possibilities for sharing and integration into other documents and applications.

This feature extends its reach across supported models and seamlessly integrates into Safari, Quick Look, and beyond.

1) Immerse yourself in a full-screen photo or halt a clip at any frame.
2) Embrace the subject with a gentle touch and hold. As an outline envelops the subject, unleash its potential:

a) Continue to caress the subject, then seamlessly transfer it into another document.
b) Tap "Copy" to preserve the subject's essence, ready to be pasted into emails, text messages, or notes.
c) Engage "Look Up" to delve deeper into the subject's realm, unveiling insights and information.
d) Enhance your visual storytelling with "Add Sticker," saving the subject as a dynamic sticker for photos, emails, or text messages.
e) Harness the strength of sharing by tapping "Share" and selecting from a plethora of options such as AirDrop, Messages, or Mail.

CHAPTER 6: BOOKS

DISCOVERING AND ENJOYING BOOKS AND AUDIOBOOKS ON YOUR IPAD

In the Books app on your iPad, you'll uncover today's hottest titles, explore curated lists by Apple Books editors, and dive into immersive series and genres. Once you've selected a book or audiobook, diving into your reading or listening experience is just a tap away.

1. **Navigate to the Books App:** Open the Books app on your iPad to get started.

2. **Explore Your Options:** Rotate your iPad to landscape view or tap to automatically access the sidebar.

3. **Find What You Want:** Head to the Book Store or Audiobook Store to browse through a wide range of titles. If you have something specific in mind, simply tap Search and enter the title, author, series, or genre.

Pro Tip: Easily navigate through sections like Top Charts and Book Clubs by tapping Browse Sections at the top of your screen. Explore genres such as Biographies & Memoirs and Young Adults for tailored recommendations.

4. **Explore Further:** Tap on a book cover to delve deeper. You can access more details, read a sample, listen to a preview, or add it to your "Want to Read" list.

5. **Making Your Selection:** When you're ready, tap "Buy" to make a purchase or "Get" to download a free title directly to your iPad.

All transactions are securely processed using the payment method linked to your Apple ID.

For iPads with cellular capability, take advantage of the ease of automatic downloads even when Wi-Fi isn't available. Simply navigate to **Settings** > **Books**, enable **Automatic Downloads**, and set your preferences under **Downloads**.

MASTERING BOOK READING IN THE BOOKS APPLICATION ON YOUR IPAD

Within the Books application, you have full control over your reading experience—from managing your current reads to organizing collections and more.

Exploring Your Reading World

Within the Books app, you can effortlessly navigate through your reading journey:

1) **Home:** Access your current reads, audiobooks, and PDFs. Receive Tailored recommendations for your subsequent reading and maintain a record of books you want to read. Establish daily reading objectives and monitor your yearly reading accomplishments.

2) **Library:** Explore all your books, series, PDFs, audiobooks, and samples. Organize them into collections like "Want to Read," "Finished," and "Downloaded." Easily manage content acquired from the Book Store or added manually.

3) **My Collections:** Create and manage custom collections to arrange your books exactly how you like. Learn how to create collections for seamless organization.

DIVING INTO READING: A STEP-BY-STEP GUIDE

To immerse yourself in a book using the Books application on your iPad, follow these simple steps:

1) **Navigate to Your Bookshelf:** Tap ▢ or rotate your iPad to landscape mode to reveal the sidebar. From there, select a category like "Home," "Books," or "Audiobooks."

2) **Open Your Book:** Find the book you like to read and tap its cover to access it.

3) **Reading Controls:** Once inside your book, you can:

   a) **Turn Pages:** Select the right margin or glide from the right side to the left to progress through the book.

Pro Tip: Customize your reading experience by enabling

Both Margins Advance in **Settings** ⚙ > **Books** to turn pages from either side.

   b) **Navigate Back:** Select the left margin or glide from the left side to the right to backtrack to the previous page.

   c) **Return to Previous Location:** Select the page and then select the rounded arrow in the upper-left edge to backtrack to your previous reading position. Select the rounded arrow in the upper-right edge to proceed back to your recent spot.

d) **Navigate to Specific Locations:** Press the page, press • • •then tap the search icon. Input a phrase, word, or page number to jump directly to your desired spot in the book.

e) **Utilize the Table of Contents:** Press the page, press• • •, then select "Contents" to access the book's table of contents. For quick navigation, touch and hold "Contents," then move your finger from side to side to swiftly move through the book.

f) **Close Your Book:** When you're done reading, tap the page and select the close icon in the upper-right corner, or simply slide downwards from the page's top to close the book.

Tap to go back to previous reading location.

Tap to close book.

Tap to navigate the table of contents, change the display, search, share, and add bookmarks.

1) **Adjust Text and Page Settings:** Press the page, press ⚉, then tap the menu icon at the bottom. Select "Themes & Settings," and from there:

   a) **Modify Font Size:** Press the large "A" to increase or the small "A" to decrease the font size according to your preference.

   b) **Enable Vertical Scrolling:** Tap the vertical scrolling icon to switch to vertical scrolling mode for a smoother reading experience.

   For PDFs, tap the menu icon AA at the upper part of the display, then enable Vertical Scrolling for easier navigation through documents.

   c) **Change Page Turn Style:** Press the menu icon, then select your preferred page turn style from the options available.

   d) **Modify Background Color:** Tap the menu icon, then pick a background color that suits your reading environment.

   e) **Adjust Display Brightness:** Touch and drag the brightness bar to modify the screen brightness to your comfort level.

   f) **Select Page Theme:** Explore different page themes like Quiet or Bold to enhance readability and atmosphere.

Font and Text Customization

   g) **Change Font:** Tap "Customize," then select "Font." Preview different font styles like Original or Palatino, and tap "Done" to apply your selection.

h) **Bold Text:** Enhance readability by toggling on Bold Text. Tap "Customize," activate Bold Text, then tap "Done" to apply.

i) **Personalize Spacing and Justification:** Press "Customize," navigate to **Accessibility & Layout Options**, and enable customization. Modify character spacing, line spacing, and word spacing using the sliders. You can also toggle Justify Text on or off for optimal reading comfort. Tap "Done" to save your changes.

2) **Close the Book:** Press the page, then press the close icon ⊗ within the upper-right edge. Alternatively, slide downwards from the page's top. (Note: Swipe down is not accessible if vertical scrolling is enabled.)

Tap to change the font and customize Accessibility & Layout options.

3) **Customize Reading Menu Position:** Adjust the position of the menu button ⋯ on the screen. Navigate to **Settings** ⊙ > press **Books**, then select "Left" or "Right" underneath Reading Menu Position.

4) **Reset Text and Layout Customizations:** If you wish to revert text and layout changes, tap the menu icon⬛••, select "Customize," then tap "Reset Theme."

BOOKMARKING YOUR PLACE

When using the Books application on your iPad, bookmark pages to easily return to them later:

1) **Bookmark a Page:** Press the page, hit⬛••, then select the bookmark icon⬗. Press it once more to delete the bookmark.

2) **Access Bookmarks:** To view all your bookmarks, press the page, select the menu icon⬛••, select "Bookmarks & Highlights," then tap "Bookmarks."

SHARING TEXT AND BOOK LINKS

Within the Books application on your iPad, you can easily share text selections or book links with others:

1) **Adjust Text Selection:** Tap and keep holding a word, then alter the grab points to pick the desired text.

2) **Share Text Selection:** After selecting the text, tap "Share." Choose from options like Mail, Messages, or other apps to distribute the selected text. If the book originates from the Book Store, a hyperlink to the book is automatically included with the text selection. (Note: Sharing Availability may differ depending on your location.)

3) **Share a Book Link:** To distribute a hyperlink for accessing the book in the Book Store:

a) Press on the page, followed by selecting the menu symbol ▤ • • •.

b) Select "Share ⬆," then choose your preferred method for distributing the hyperlink (via AirDrop, Mail, Messages, etc.).

MASTERING ANNOTATION IN THE BOOKS APPLICATION ON IPAD

Highlight, Underline, and Take Notes Effortlessly

In the Books app 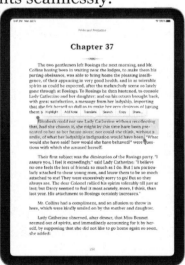 on your iPad, you have the power to enrich your reading experience through annotations. Whether you're a beginner or seasoned user, annotating text allows you to engage deeply with your books and share your insights seamlessly.

HOW TO HIGHLIGHT OR UNDERLINE TEXT:

1. **Open Your Book:** Launch the Books app and select the book you're reading.
2. **Select Your Text:** Touch and hold any word, then adjust the selection by moving the grab points.
3. **Highlight with Ease:** Tap "Highlight" to mark the selected text. For underlining, tap the text again, choose "Highlight," and then select "Underline" from the options.

Managing Your Annotations:

a) **Editing and Removal:** To modify or remove a highlight or underline, press the annotated text and select the appropriate option.
b) **Reviewing Annotations:** Easily access all your highlights by tapping the page, press ● ● ●, navigating to "Bookmarks & Highlights," and selecting "Highlights." Each highlight links directly to its corresponding location within the book, simplifying navigation.

HOW TO HIGHLIGHT, UNDERLINE, AND ADD NOTES:

1. **Open Your Book:** Launch the Books app and select the book you're reading.
2. **Annotate Text:** Touch and hold any word, then adjust the selection using the grab points.
3. **Highlight or Underline:** Press "Highlight" to mark text. To underline, press the text again, choose "Highlight," then select "Underline."

4. **Add Notes:** Tap "Add Note," enter your text, and tap "Done." To delete a note, press the text and select "Delete Note."

Managing Your Annotations:

a) **Review Annotations:** Access all your highlights and notes by tapping the page, press • • •, navigating to "Bookmarks & Highlights," and selecting "Highlights." Each annotation is linked directly to its location within the book for easy reference.

SHARING HIGHLIGHTS AND NOTES:

1. **Open Your Book:** Navigate to the book where you've stored highlights or notes.

2. **Access Annotations:** Press any page, press • • •, then tap "Bookmarks & Highlights," followed by "Highlights."

3. **Share Your Insights:** Press and maintain your touch on the highlighted text or note you wish to distribute, then select "Share ⬆." For multiple annotations, tap "Select ✓," choose the items, and then tap "Share ⬆."

4. **Choose Your Method:** Select a sharing option like AirDrop, Messages, or Mail to share your annotations.

5. **Complete Sharing:** After sharing, tap "Done" to close "Bookmarks & Highlights."

HOW TO ERASE NOTES, HIGHLIGHTS, AND BOOKMARKS:

1) **Open Your Book:** Launch the Books app and navigate to the book where you've stored notes, highlights, or bookmarks.

2) **Access Annotations:** Tap any page, touch ⋯, then touch the ellipsis icon (...) and select "Bookmarks & Highlights." Choose either "Bookmarks" or "Highlights."

3) **Delete Individual Annotations:**
   a) **Single Item:** Press and sustain your touch on the bookmark, highlighted text, or note you like to remove, then select "Delete 🗑."
   b) **Multiple Items:** Touch and hold any Object you like to remove, select "Select ✓," choose the elements you like to remove, then select the trash can icon 🗑.

4) **Complete the Process:** Tap "Done" to close "Bookmarks & Highlights" once you've finished deleting items.

MASTERING BOOK ACCESS ACROSS APPLE DEVICES IN BOOKS ON IPAD

Syncing Your Reading Experience Effortlessly
Discover the convenience of accessing your favorite books and audiobooks seamlessly across all your Apple devices using the Books application. Whether you're switching between your iPad, iPhone, or MacBook,

239

syncing ensures you never lose your place or your annotations.

HOW TO ACCESS YOUR BOOKS ON ADDITIONAL APPLE DEVICES:

Ensure your reading experience stays consistent and up-to-date across all your Apple devices by following these simple steps:

1) **Sync Purchases Automatically:**
   a) Navigate to **Settings** > press **Books** on each device.
   b) Enable **Purchases from Other Devices** to automatically download your purchases across all devices. Ensure the toggle is green to activate.

2) **Sync Reading Position and Annotations:**
   a) Navigate to **Settings** > press **[Your Name]** > **iCloud** > **iCloud Drive**.
   b) Enable **Sync this iPad** and ensure **Books** is enabled under **Show All** to synchronize your notes, bookmarks, reading position, and highlights seamlessly.

3) **Synchronize Library, Home, and Collections:**
   a) In **Settings**, navigate to **Books**.
   b) Below **Syncing**, enable **Home** and **iCloud Drive** to synchronize your library collections across devices. Confirm the toggle is green to activate.

ACCESSING YOUR BOOKS ON YOUR MACBOOK: A COMPREHENSIVE GUIDE

Syncing Your Audiobooks, Books, and PDFs Effortlessly

Explore the smooth incorporation of your reading materials across devices by accessing your Books app content on your Mac. Whether you're using the latest macOS version or an earlier one, syncing ensures your notes, bookmarks, collections, and highlights are readily accessible to you.

How to Retrieve Your Books on Your MacBook:
Ensure your Books content is available on your Mac by adhering to these instructions based on your macOS version:

1) **For macOS 13 and Subsequent Versions:**

    a) Navigate to **Apple menu** > press **System Settings**.

    b) Click on your **name** in the side panel, followed by choosing iCloud on the right side.

    c) Click **iCloud Drive** and navigate to **Applications synchronizing to iCloud Drive**.

    d) Select **Books**, then click **Back** and **Done**. If you're not signed in, hit **Sign in with your Apple ID** to input your credentials.

2) **macOS 10.15–12.5:**

    a) Select **Apple menu** >press **System Preferences**.

    b) Click **Apple ID**, then select **iCloud** within the sidebar.

    c) Click **Options** next to **iCloud Drive**, then pick **Books**.

3) **macOS 10.14 or older versions:**

    a) Select Apple menu >press System Preferences.

    b) Click **iCloud**, then pick **iCloud Drive**.

    c) Click **Options**, then choose **Books**.

Viewing Your Notes, Bookmarks, Collections, and Highlights on Your MacBook:
Ensure all your annotations and organizational preferences are synced to your Mac by adhering to these instructions:
1) **For macOS 13 and Subsequent Versions:**
   a) Open **Books** and pick **Books** > press **Settings**.
   b) Hit **General**, then pick **Collections, bookmarks, and highlights**.
2) **macOS 12.5 and prior versions:**
   a) Open **Books** and pick **Books** > press **Preferences**.
   b) Hit **General**, then pick **Collections, bookmarks, and highlights**.

DISCOVER THE JOY OF AUDIOBOOKS ON YOUR IPAD

START LISTENING EFFORTLESSLY WITH THE BOOKS APP

1) **Launch Your Audiobook**

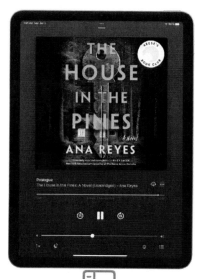

a) Begin by tapping on your iPad or simply rotate it to landscape mode for easy sidebar access.

b) Navigate to the "Audiobooks," "All," or "Home" tab within the Books app. Locate your desired audiobook and tap its cover to start playback.

2) **Enjoy Seamless Playback**

a) Once your audiobook is playing, you have full control:

i) **Navigate Through Content:** Skip forward or backward by tapping the rounded arrows near the pause button or utilize external controls like headphones.

ii) **Jump to a Specific Point:** Drag the slider beneath the audiobook cover to adjust playback time.

iii) **Adjust Volume:** Easily fine-tune volume levels by moving the slider adjacent to the pause button.

iv) **Adjust Playback Speed:** Tailor your listening pace by tapping the speed of playback (1x) located at the bottom left and selecting your preferred speed.

v) **Set a Sleep Timer:** Ensure a restful night by tapping 🌙, then choosing a duration for your audiobook to play.

vi) **Switch Devices Seamlessly:** Move your audiobook playback to another device like Apple TV, HomePod, or Bluetooth® speakers by tapping 📶 and selecting an available device.

vii) **Navigate Easily:** Explore different sections of your audiobook by tapping ☰ , then selecting a chapter (also known as tracks in some audiobooks).

viii) **Maximize Screen Space:** Transition to the compact audiobook player effortlessly by tapping ▬ or swiping Down at any location on the display to return to full Screen, hit the bottom-located mini-player.

ix) **Manage Playback:** Shut the audiobook player by tapping ▬ , or long-press the mini-player, then hit Close Audio Player.

Stay Connected Anywhere

If Wi-Fi isn't available, your audiobooks can still play over your cellular network, though this may incur additional fees. Manage data usage by adjusting settings in Inspect or modify the cellular data configurations on iPad (Wi-Fi + Cellular models).

Certain audiobooks include supplemental PDFs. Locate these files by tapping••• underneath the audiobook cover in your collection, subsequently tapping View PDF Content.

ACHIEVE YOUR READING GOALS WITH EASE ON IPAD

Master Your Reading Journey with the Books App

The Books application📖 on iPad empowers you to track your daily reading minutes, book completions, and audiobook achievements effortlessly. Customize your goals to boost your reading time, establish new streaks, and receive motivating prompts to assist you achieve your targets.

1) **Adjust Your Reading Goal:** Personalize Your Everyday Reading Objective based on your preferred reading time. By default, it's configured for 5 minutes daily.

   a) Begin by tapping or switching to landscape view to access the sidebar.

   b) Navigate to Home and locate the reading objectives icon in the upper right corner.

   c) Select the reading goal timer, followed by select Adjust Goal.

   d) Use the slider to set your desired daily reading minutes.

Enhance Your Reading Experience

a) **Include PDFs in Your Goals:** To track PDFs in your reading progress, navigate to **Settings** > press **Books**, and enable **Include PDFs**.

CUSTOMIZE YOUR YEARLY READING GOAL ON IPAD

Manage Your Reading Journey

Unlock the power of setting and achieving your yearly reading goals with the intuitive features of the Books application on your iPad. Whether you're aiming to read more books or simply enjoy tracking your progress, the Books app makes it effortless to tailor your goals and stay motivated.

Adjust Your Yearly Reading Goal

1) **Personalize Your Goal:** Modify your yearly reading goal based on the number of books you wish to complete.

a) Start by tapping ⬒ or switching to landscape view to access the sidebar.
b) Navigate to Home and locate the reading objectives icon in the upper right corner.
c) Select a book cover or placeholder under "Books Read This Year," then tap Adjust Goal.
d) Use the slider to set your desired number of books per year, then tap **Done**.

Streamline Your Reading Experience

a) **Mark Books as Finished:** Once you've completed a book or audiobook, maintain an organized library by marking it as finished. Tap ••• next to the book or audiobook cover, then select **Mark as Finished**.

STAY MOTIVATED WITH COACHING NOTIFICATIONS ON IPAD

Receive Personalized Encouragement

Harness the power of coaching notifications in the Books application on your iPad to stay motivated and on track towards your reading goals. Whether you're aiming to read more consistently or striving to achieve specific milestones, coaching notifications provide gentle reminders and encouragement along your reading journey.

Enable Coaching Notifications

1) **Activate Your Notifications:** Begin by tapping ⬒ or switching to landscape view to access the sidebar.
   a) Navigate to Home, then tap your account button located in the top right corner.
   b) Select Notifications, then toggle on Coaching.
   c) Tap **Done** to confirm your settings.

Tailor Your Notification Preferences

1) **Adjust Goal Completion Notifications:** Books app notifies you upon achieving a reading goal or setting a reading streak. You can customize these notifications.

   a) Tap or switch to landscape view to access the sidebar.
   b) Navigate to Home, afterwards select your account button within the upper-right edge.
   c) Select Notifications, then toggle off Goal Completion.
   d) Tap **Done** to save your changes.

FINE-TUNE YOUR READING EXPERIENCE

a) **Switch Off Reading Goals:** Navigate to **Settings** > press **Books**, and disable Reading Goals to hide reading indicators in Home and opt out of reading notifications.

RESET YOUR READING DATA

a) **Erase Reading Goals Data:** To initialize reading data like hours dedicated to reading, reading objectives, and streaks, move to **Settings** > press **Books**, afterwards select **Clear Reading Goals Data**.

MASTERING BOOK ORGANIZATION IN THE BOOKS APPLICATION ON IPAD: A SIMPLE GUIDE

Effortlessly Organize Your Digital Library

The Books application on your iPad is designed to safeguard your books and audiobooks neatly organized. By default, your purchases are sorted into collections like Audiobooks, Want to Read, and Finished. But did you know you can customize these collections to better suit your reading habits?

CREATING YOUR CUSTOM COLLECTIONS

Personalizing your library with custom collections is a great way to safeguard your books organized just the way you like. Here's how you can do it:

1. **Launch the Books App:** Open the Books app on your iPad.
2. **Access the Sidebar:** Tap the sidebar icon, or rotate your iPad to landscape mode to automatically reveal the sidebar.
3. **Initiate a New Collection:** Tap "New Collection" to start creating your custom category.
4. **Name Your Collection:** Enter a name for your new collection, such as "Beach Reads" or "Book Club," and then tap "Done."

ADDING BOOKS TO YOUR COLLECTIONS

After you have configured your collections, you can start populating them with your favorite books. Here's how:

1. **Launch the Books Application:** Start by launching the Books application on your iPad.

2. **Access Your Books:** Tap the sidebar icon or rotate your iPad to landscape view. Then choose "Book Store" or "Library" to browse your books.

3. **Select a Book:** Touch the book cover to view more details.

4. **Add to a Collection:** Tap "Add to Collection" and choose the collection you wish to add the book to.

Pro Tip: You can add the same book to multiple collections, so feel free to categorize it in different ways that make sense to you.

ADJUSTING DISPLAY AND SORTING OPTIONS

Tailoring the way your books are shown and sorted can make it easier to find what you're looking for. Follow these simple steps:

1) **Launch the Books Application:** Launch the Books application on your iPad.

2) **Reveal the Sidebar:** Tap the sidebar icon or rotate your iPad to landscape mode to access the sidebar.

3) **Select a Category:** Tap a category under "Library" or "My Collections."

4) **Modify Display and Order:**
   a) **Change Display:** Tap "Grid" or "List" to choose how your books are shown.
   b) **Change Order:** Tap "Recent," "Title," "Author," or "Manual" to sort your books. If you select "Manual," Press and grip a book cover, afterwards move it to rearrange its position.

REMOVING OR HIDING AUDIOBOOKS, BOOKS, AND PDFS

If you need to clean up your library by removing or hiding certain items, here's how to do it:

1. **Launch the Books Application:** Start by opening the Books application on your iPad.

2. **Access the Sidebar:** Tap the sidebar icon or rotate your iPad to landscape mode.

3. **Select and Remove:** Tap "Home" or a specific collection under "Library." Then, tap the ellipsis adjacent to the title you wish to remove.

4) **Choose Your Option:**
   a) **Remove Download:** Select "Remove Download" to delete the content and data linked with the title from your iPad. To reacquire it later, simply tap the download icon.
   b) **Hide Book:** Choose "Hide Book" to make the book disappear from your library and collections. To unhide, tap "Home," then your account icon, and select "Manage Hidden Purchases."

Automatically Remove Downloads After Finishing a Book

To keep your iPad uncluttered, you can set it to automatically remove downloads once you finish reading:

1. **Launch the Books Application:** Start by opening the Books application on your iPad.

2. **Access Collections:** Tap a collection under "Library," then tap the ellipsis on the screen's upper side.

3. **Set Automatic Removal:** Tap "Remove Downloads," then choose "Automatically When Finished."

DELETING A COLLECTION

If you need to remove a whole collection, follow these steps:

1. **Launch the Books Application:** Tap the sidebar icon or rotate your iPad to landscape mode to see your collections.
2. **Select and Delete:** Under "My Collections," Slide left on the collection you like to remove, then select "Delete."

Please Note: Removing a collection does not remove the books or audiobooks contained within it; those remain in your library.

EFFORTLESS PDF MANAGEMENT WITH THE BOOKS APPLICATION ON YOUR IPAD

Discover the Ease of Reading, Sharing, and Marking Up PDFs

The Books application on your iPad provides a user-friendly way to handle PDFs you receive through various apps like Mail and Messages. Regardless of whether you wish to read, share, or annotate your PDFs, you'll find the process both straightforward and efficient. Here's how to maximize the benefits of your PDFs with just a few taps:

OPENING PDFS IN THE BOOKS APP

Reading PDFs on your iPad is simple and convenient. Adhere to these instructions to open and save PDFs in the Books app:

1. **Open the PDF:** Tap the PDF file you wish to view.

2. **Share the PDF:** Tap the share icon (usually a square with an arrow pointing up).

3. **Save to Books:** From the list of sharing options, select "Books" to open and save the PDF in your Books app library.

SHARING OR PRINTING A PDF

If you need to share or print a PDF, the Books app makes it easy:

1. **Open the PDF:** Tap the PDF file to view it.

2. **Access Share Options:** Tap the share icon, then choose how you'd like to share the PDF—options include AirDrop, Mail, Messages, or printing. For printing, refer to the Apple Support article on AirPrint for more details.

MARKING UP A PDF

Annotating PDFs is an excellent method to highlight important information or make notes. Here's how to utilize the markup tools:

1. **Open the PDF:** Start by pressing on the PDF to view it.

2. **Access Markup Tools:** Select the markup icon (usually a pen or pencil icon). If it doesn't appear right away, tap near the center of the page to reveal the tool options.

CHAPTER 7: MASTERING FACETIME ON YOUR IPAD

DISCOVER THE EASE OF CONNECTING FACE-TO-FACE

FaceTime  on your iPad opens up a world of effortless communication with friends and family, whether you're on Wi-Fi or cellular data. Imagine having the ability to catch up with loved ones, watch TV shows and movies together, listen to music, or even share a workout session—all from the comfort of your home. FaceTime makes staying connected easy and enjoyable.

SETTING UP FACETIME: A SIMPLE START

Getting started with FaceTime is a breeze. Simply adhere to these instructions:

1. Launch the Settings application on your iPad.

2. Navigate to **FaceTime** and switch it on.
3. If you haven't already, log in utilizing your Apple ID to activate FaceTime.

MAKING YOUR FIRST FACETIME CALL

To initiate a FaceTime call:

1. Launch the **FaceTime** application.
2. Tap on **New FaceTime**.
3. Input the name or phone number of the individual you like to reach.

You can pick between a video call by selecting the camera icon or an audio call (available in selected regions). FaceTime supports group calls featuring a maximum of 32 participants, so you can easily connect with several individuals simultaneously

If you need to reach someone who doesn't own an Apple device, you can still include them in your call. Simply create and share a call link through **Messages** or **Mail**. To do this, open the FaceTime app and select **Create Link** to get started.

Turn your mic on or off.

Turn your camera
on or off.

UTILIZING FACETIME CONTROLS: ENHANCING YOUR CALL EXPERIENCE

Master the FaceTime Controls for a Seamless Conversation

When you're on a FaceTime call, you have a variety of controls at your fingertips to customize your experience. If you don't immediately see these controls, simply tap your screen to reveal them. You can easily turn your speaker, microphone, or camera on or off, and manage other settings to suit your needs.

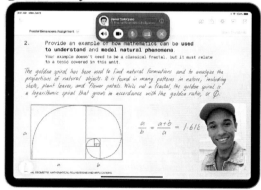

SHARE YOUR SCREEN WHILE ON A FACETIME CALL

One of the standout features of FaceTime is the capability to share your display with other participants. This is the way to do it:

1. While engaged in a call, tap the **FaceTime controls** (In case you don't find the controls, tap your screen).
2. Select **Share My Screen**.
3. Navigate to your **Home Screen** and open the app or document you like to share. A brief glimpse of your screen will appear in the call window.

Participants can tap on this preview to enlarge and view your content in detail. This feature is perfect for sharing presentations, showing photos, or collaborating on documents in real-time.

Explore More FaceTime Features

To maximize the benefits of your FaceTime experience, consider exploring the following:

a) Adding more people to your FaceTime call.
b) Managing participants and viewing them in a grid layout.
c) Adjusting your FaceTime video and audio settings for the best quality.
d) Remember, not all features and content may be available in every country or region.

MAKING AND RECEIVING FACETIME CALLS: A SIMPLE GUIDE

EFFORTLESS COMMUNICATION WITH FACETIME ON YOUR IPAD

FaceTime makes connecting with loved ones easier than ever. With just online access and your Apple ID, you can quickly Initiate and accept FaceTime calls right from your iPad. Before you start, ensure FaceTime is set up on your device. If you're using an iPad with Wi-Fi + Cellular, you can also make calls over a cellular data connection—though this may involve additional charges. If you'd rather to use Wi-Fi only, you can disable cellular FaceTime calls by navigating to **Settings** > press **Cellular** and turning off FaceTime.

How to Make a FaceTime Call

Getting started with a FaceTime call is straightforward:

1. Launch the **FaceTime** application on your iPad.
2. Tap **New FaceTime** located Adjacent to the Screen's Top.
3. Type the name or phone number of the person you like to reach in the entry field on the screen's upper side.
4. Press the **video camera symbol** to initiate a video call, or the **phone icon** for a FaceTime audio call (note that audio calls Might Not Be Accessible in Every Geographic Location).

If you prefer, you can press the **Contacts** icon to browse through your contacts and start a call directly from there. Alternatively, you can choose a contact from your call history for a quick and convenient call.

Want to include more people in your call? Check out the section on **Making a Group FaceTime Call on iPad**. For even more convenience, you can use Siri to place your call. Simply say something like, "Make a FaceTime call" or "Call Eliza's mobile." For details on using Siri, refer to the Siri guide.

Tip: To get a better view during your FaceTime video call, rotate your iPad to landscape orientation. This will give you a wider perspective and improve your video call experience. For instructions on how to modify or lock the screen orientation, see the relevant section in your iPad's settings.

How To Create a Video Note

If your FaceTime video call goes unanswered, you can create a Video Note to ensure your message gets through. This is the way to do it:

1. Tap **Record Video**. A Countdown from 5 to 1 Will Be Displayed, Allowing You Some Time to Get Ready.

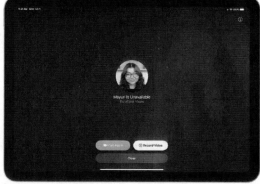

2. Once the countdown ends, record your message. When you're finished, tap the **send icon** ⬆ to send your video message. If you're not satisfied with your

recording, tap **Retake** to try again. You can also tap **Save** to store the video in your Photos app for later. After sending your video message, the recipient will be notified of your message.

Note: Video Messages Can Solely acquire from Contacts in Your Saved List, individuals you've called, or Individuals proposed by Siri. For more information on how to listen to video or audio messages, refer to the relevant section in your guide.

Leaving a Voicemail on FaceTime

If the recipient doesn't answer the FaceTime audio call has Live Voicemail enabled, you will be instructed to leave a voicemail. This feature is accessible through **Settings** > **Phone** on an iPhone that's signed into FaceTime utilizing identical Apple ID as their iPad.

Note: Live Voicemail is currently available only in English in the U.S. (excluding Puerto Rico) and Canada.

Quickly Redialing a FaceTime Call

In case you need to call someone again via FaceTime, you can do so easily with a few simple actions:

a) On the **Record Video** screen, tap **Call Again**.

b) Alternatively, open your **call history** and tap the name or number of the individual (or group) you wish to call again.

These quick options make it effortless to reconnect without having to search through your contacts.

Initiating a FaceTime Call from Messages

You can seamlessly initiate a FaceTime call directly from an iMessage conversation. Follow these steps:

1. Open the iMessage conversation with the person you want to call.

2. Tap the **FaceTime icon** at the upper right of the screen.

3. Choose between **FaceTime Audio** or **FaceTime Video** to initiate your call.

Important: Should you be operating on iPadOS 17.4 or a later version and have deleted the FaceTime app from your iPad, or if FaceTime was removed in a previous iPadOS version, reinstallation of the app will be necessary to initiate or accept FaceTime calls. and join SharePlay sessions. Without the app, your settings and contact cards related to FaceTime won't be visible.

MASTERING FACETIME: HOW TO EFFORTLESSLY ANSWER CALLS ON YOUR IPAD

Welcoming Incoming FaceTime Calls: A Simple Guide

Receiving a FaceTime call on your iPad is straightforward and user-friendly. This is the way to handle those incoming calls with ease:

1. **Answering the Call:** When engaged in a FaceTime call arrives, you have a few options to connect. Simply move the slider or press on **Accept** or **Join** to answer the call.

2. **Declining the Call**: If you're not available to take the call, tap **Decline** or the red **X** icon to politely refuse the call.

3. **Setting a Reminder**: If you like to return the call later, tap **Remind Me**. This will help you remember to call back at a more convenient time.

4. **Sending a Quick Message**: To let the caller know you're currently unavailable, you can tap **Message** to forward them a quick note.

Handling Calls During Another Call

If you're already on another call when a FaceTime call comes in, you'll see an option to **End & Accept**. This permits you to terminate your ongoing call and switch to the incoming FaceTime session seamlessly.

Pro Tip: To make managing your calls even easier, you can enable Siri to announce incoming FaceTime calls. This way, you can accept or decline calls just by using your voice, making the process even more convenient.

Listening to Video and Audio Messages Made Simple

If you ever miss a FaceTime call, you have easy ways to update oneself on missed messages:

1. **Viewing Video Messages**: In case you overlook a video call from a known contact and they Drop a video message, you'll receive a notification. Tap the notification to view the message. Alternatively, you can locate the video link in your FaceTime call history right underneath the missed call entry.

2. **Accessing Audio Messages**: For missed audio calls, if you have Live Voicemail activated on your iPhone (signed in utilizing identical Apple ID as your iPad), the caller can leave a voicemail. Make sure to check your voicemail settings under **Settings** > **Phone** on your iPhone.

Important Note: You can only receive video messages from saved contacts, people you've previously called, or individuals suggested by Siri.

A recorded video message

A recorded voicemail

Managing Your Call History

To keep your call history organized, you might like to delete calls that are no longer relevant:

1. **Deleting a Call**: Access the FaceTime application , find the call If you wish to delete, glide left on the call entry, and then hit the red **Delete** button

EFFORTLESSLY CREATE AND SHARE FACETIME LINKS ON YOUR IPAD

How to Generate a FaceTime Link for Seamless Video Calls

Creating and sharing a FaceTime link on your iPad is a quick and simple way to connect with friends, family, or colleagues. This is the way to easily set up a FaceTime link and make scheduling remote meetings a breeze:

1. **Generate a FaceTime Link**: Access the FaceTime application 🎥 on your iPad, as well as tap **Create Link** located on the screen's upper side. This action generates a unique link that you can utilize to start or join a FaceTime call.

2. **Send the Link**: After creating the link, choose your preferred method for sending it, such as **Mail**, **Messages**, or another communication app. Share the link with individuals or groups to invite them to the call.

3. **Schedule Meetings in Calendar**: If you're organizing a remote video meeting, you can insert the FaceTime link into the **Calendar** app as the meeting location. This facilitates seamless for participants to join the video call directly from their calendar event.

Important Note: You can invite anyone to join your FaceTime call, even if they don't have an Apple device. They can participate in one-on-one or Group FaceTime sessions from their web browser. Just ensure they have the latest update of Chrome or Edge and support for H.264 video encoding for video calls.

CAPTURE MEMORABLE MOMENTS: HOW TO TAKE A LIVE PHOTO WITHIN FACETIME ON YOUR IPAD

Easily Capture a Live Photo During Your FaceTime Calls

Capturing special moments during your FaceTime calls is a breeze with the Live Photo feature on your iPad. This permits you to record a snapshot of your conversation, including the moments before and after, complete with audio. Here's a sequential roadmap to help you take a Live Photo effortlessly:

1) **Enable FaceTime Live Photos**: First, ensure that FaceTime Live Photos is activated. Navigate to Settings ⚙ > **FaceTime** On your iPad, as well as toggle the feature on.

2) **Taking a Live Photo During a Call**:
   a) **One-on-One Call**: While on a video call with a single person, simply tap the **Live Photo** button ◯ (a white circle with a starburst) to capture the moment.
   b) **Group FaceTime Call**: If you're engaged in a Group FaceTime call, tap on the tile of the person you want to photograph, then tap the **Live Photo** button ◯ (a white circle with a starburst).

3) **Notifications and Saving**: Both you and the person you're calling will be notified when your iPad takes a Live Photo. Live Photos are automatically saved in your **Photos** app, where you can revisit the captured moment anytime.

Important Note: FaceTime Live Photos might not be accessible in every geographical area.

ENHANCE YOUR FACETIME EXPERIENCE: HOW TO ENABLE LIVE CAPTIONS ON YOUR IPAD

Turning On Live Captions for Clearer Conversations

If you're having trouble hearing during a FaceTime video call, Live Captions can be a valuable tool. This feature converts spoken words into text, which appears in real time on your iPad screen. Here's how to activate and use Live Captions to make your conversations more accessible and engaging:

1. **Activate Live Captions**: While on a FaceTime call, hit the screen to reveal the FaceTime options if they aren't already visible. Next, tap the **Live Captions** icon ⓘ at the upper part of the controls to turn on the feature. Then, hit **Done** to start displaying captions.

2. **Viewing Live Captions**: Once enabled, a Live Captions window will be visible at the upper part of your display. This window shows the dialogue from the call, automatically transcribed, and indicates who is speaking, making it easier for you to follow the conversation.

3. **Turning Off Live Captions**: If you like to stop displaying captions, tap the screen again, access the FaceTime controls, tap the **Live Captions** icon ⓘ, and then switch off the feature.

Important Considerations: Live Captions can be accessed on compatible iPad models when the Language preference is configured to American English or Canadian English. Please note that the precision of Live Captions can vary, so it may not be suitable for high-risk or emergency situations. Additionally, using Live Captions may consume extra battery power.

MASTER MULTITASKING: USING OTHER APPLICATIONS DURING A FACETIME CALL ON YOUR IPAD

Effortless Integration of Communication and Productivity

FaceTime calls on your iPad are not only an excellent method to remain connected, but they also offer the flexibility to multitask efficiently. Whether you're looking to look up important information, jot down notes, or perform quick calculations, you can easily switch between FaceTime and other apps without missing a beat.

Navigating Between Apps Seamlessly

While you're engaged in a FaceTime session, you can seamlessly use other apps. Simply navigate to your Home Screen by swiping up from the screen's base. Once there, tap the icon of the app you wish to use. Your FaceTime call will continue in the background, allowing you to manage your tasks with ease.

Returning to Your FaceTime Call

To return to your FaceTime call after using another app, just tap the green bar on the screen's upper side. This bar will either display as green or show the FaceTime icon, in accordance with your iPad model. A single tap on this bar will bring you back to your FaceTime conversation instantly.

Sharing Your Screen During the Call

In addition to multitasking, you can also share your screen with the participants in your FaceTime call while using another app. This feature allows everyone on the call to see exactly what's on your screen. For more details on how to share your screen, refer to the section "Share Your Screen in a FaceTime Call."

CHAPTER 8: SEAMLESSLY CONNECT WITH EVERYONE: HOW TO INITIATE A GROUP FACETIME CALL ON YOUR IPAD

Bringing Multiple Voices Together with Ease

Making a Group FaceTime call on your iPad allows you to connect featuring a maximum of 32 participants, making it perfect for family gatherings, team meetings, or catching up with friends. Whether you're new to FaceTime or a seasoned user, this guide will help you set up your group call effortlessly.

STARTING YOUR GROUP FACETIME CALL

1. **Access the FaceTime application:** Launch the FaceTime app on your iPad by tapping its symbol on your Home Screen.

2. **Initiate a New Call:** Once in the FaceTime app, tap "New FaceTime" located adjacent to the top of your screen. This action will prompt you to enter the details of your call.

3. **Add Participants:** In the entry field that appears at the upper part of the screen, type the names or phone numbers of the people you wish to include in the call.

   If you prefer, tap the ⊕ icon to open your Contacts list and add people from there. Alternatively, you can select suggested contacts from your call history.

4. **Choose Your Call Type:** To start a video call, tap the video camera icon ⬜◤. If you prefer a voice-only

conversation, hit the phone symbol ☏ to initiate an audio-only FaceTime call.

Effortless Interaction and Visibility During Group Calls

In a Group FaceTime call on your iPad, each participant is displayed in a tile on your screen. When someone speaks—whether verbally or through sign language—or if you tap their tile, that participant's tile will become highlighted to make them stand out. This feature helps you easily identify who is actively speaking or who you intend to focus on.

Understanding Tile Layout and Navigation

a) **Tile Visibility**: If there are more participants than can fit on your screen, tiles that don't fit will appear in a row at the lowest section of your display. To view these participants, simply slide across the row to locate the person you need.

b) **Initials and Images**: If a participant doesn't have an image available, their initials may be displayed in their tile, helping you quickly recognize them.

Adjusting Tile Prominence

If you prefer that the tile of the person speaking does not become more prominent, you can adjust this setting:

1. Open **Settings** ⚙ on your iPad.
2. Navigate to **FaceTime**.
3. Turn off the **Speaking** option below **Automatic Prominence**.

Enhanced Viewing Options

For a different viewing experience where participants' images are aligned in a grid layout, refer to the section "View Participants in a Grid Layout in FaceTime on iPad."

Compatibility Notes

To use sign language detection, both the presenter and participants need to have devices running iOS 14, iPadOS 14, macOS 11, or later. Additionally, a supported model for the presenter is required for this feature to work effectively.

INITIATE, MANAGE, AND LEAVE GROUP FACETIME CALLS WITH EASE ON YOUR IPAD

Connecting Seamlessly from Messages and Managing Participants

Group FaceTime calls are a fantastic way to bring together multiple people for conversations, whether for work or personal chats. Using your device, you can easily Initiate a Group FaceTime call within a group iMessage chat, add participants during the call, join a call you're invited to, and leave the call whenever needed.

Initiating a Group FaceTime session within a Group Messages Chat

1) **Open the Group iMessage Conversation:** Go to the group chat in the Messages application where you're conversing with multiple people.

2) **Initiate the Call:** Hit the FaceTime button found in the top right quadrant of the iMessage conversation.

3) **Choose Your Call Type**
   a) **For a Video Call**: Tap **FaceTime Video**.
   b) **For an Audio Call**: Tap **FaceTime Audio**.

Adding A different person to the Call

You can expand your call by adding new participants at any time:

1) **Show FaceTime Controls:** During an active FaceTime call, press the screen if the FaceTime controls are not visible. Hit the **Add People** symbol (i) at the upper part of the controls.

2) **Add a Participant:**

   a) **Enter Details**: Input the name, Apple ID, or phone number of the person you want to include in the entry box.

   b) **Select from Contacts**: Tap the ⊕ icon to add someone from your Contacts list.

3) **Complete the Addition:** Tap **Add People** to invite them to the call.

Joining a Group FaceTime Call

Upon receiving an invite to join a Group FaceTime call, you'll get a notification. Simply choose to join or decline based on your preference. For more details on how to answer a FaceTime call, refer to the section "Answer a FaceTime Call."

Leaving a Group FaceTime Call

To exit a Group FaceTime call:

1. **Tap Leave:** During the call, tap **Leave** to end. The call will continue if there are two or more participants remaining.

OPTIMIZE YOUR GROUP VIEW: HOW TO DISPLAY PARTICIPANTS ORGANIZED IN A GRID ON FACETIME

While in a FaceTime call with at least four attendees, switching to a grid layout can enhance your viewing experience. This layout arranges all participants in evenly sized tiles, making it easy to monitor everyone on the call.

Whether you're new to FaceTime or looking to improve your group call experience, this guide will help you set up and manage your call view effortlessly.

Activating the Grid Layout

1. **During Your Call:** When you are on a FaceTime call with multiple participants, look for the **Grid** button, which is located Adjacent to the upper right quadrant of the screen. In case you don't find the button, tap the screen to make the controls appear.

2. **Select the Grid Layout:** Tap the **Grid** button to switch your view to a grid layout. This arrangement will display all participants in evenly sized tiles, so you can see everyone at once. The tile of the active speaker will be automatically highlighted, making it easy to identify who is speaking. Note that Based on the exact version of your iPad, some tiles might appear slightly blurred.

Deactivating the Grid Layout

To revert to the default view:

1. **Tap the Grid Button Again**: Simply tap the **Grid** button once more to turn off the grid layout. Your FaceTime screen will return to the standard perspective.

EXPERIENCE SEAMLESS ENTERTAINMENT WITH SHAREPLAY ON FACETIME

Discover the Joy of Watching, Listening, and Playing Together

By utilizing SharePlay in FaceTime application, you can effortlessly stream TV shows, music, and movies in perfect sync with your friends and family while engaged in a FaceTime call. This feature ensures a real-time connection, allowing everyone on the call to experience the same moments simultaneously. Thanks to synchronized viewing and communal controls, everyone experiences the same scenes and sounds at the exact same time.

Smart Volume for Uninterrupted Conversations

One of the standout features of SharePlay is Smart Volume, which automatically adjusts the media audio to allow you to proceed chatting without missing a beat. Whether you're viewing an exciting film or listening to your preferred music the audio levels will adapt to ensure your conversations remain clear and uninterrupted.

Multiplayer Gaming Fun

SharePlay isn't just for watching and listening; you can also dive into supported multiplayer games in Game Center with your friends while engaged in a FaceTime call. This adds a whole new dimension of fun and interaction, making your calls even more engaging.

Explore More Apps with SharePlay

SharePlay extends beyond just media and games. During a FaceTime call, you can explore other applications that support SharePlay. Simply tap the **SharePlay** icon and scroll through the available apps under "Apps for SharePlay" to see what else you can enjoy together.

Important Considerations

1) Some apps that support SharePlay may require a subscription.

2) For a shared viewing experience of movies or TV shows, every participant must have the content available on their individual device, acquired either through a subscription service or a direct purchase, and meet the minimum system requirements.

3) SharePlay may not support sharing certain Cinematic or television content spanning various nations or geographical areas.

4) FaceTime, along with certain FaceTime functionalities and other services provided by Apple, Might be unavailable in every geographical area.

ENJOY CINEMA AND TV SERIES TOGETHER DURING FACETIME CALLS

Experience Shared Viewing with Ease

Watching cinematic and television content with loved ones while engaged in a FaceTime conversation has never been easier. Just adhere to these easy steps to start your shared viewing experience:

1. **Initiate a FaceTime Call**: Access the FaceTime application  on your iPad, as well as start a call with your friends or family.

2. **Select an App**: Tap the **SharePlay** icon, then pick an app from the "Listen and Play Together" section, such as the Apple TV application. Alternatively, you can navigate to the Home Screen and launch a video streaming application that is compatible with SharePlay.

3. **Choose Your Content**: Pick the show or movie you want to watch, hit the Play button, and select "Play for Everyone" if prompted. Others on the call may need to tap "Join SharePlay" to start watching.

Once all participants have the ability to view the content, specifically the video will play simultaneously for all participants. If someone doesn't have access, they'll be prompted to get it through a subscription, purchase, or free trial if available.

Control Your Viewing Experience

Each participant can use Manipulation commands to start, halt, reverse, or accelerate the video playback. Individual Configuration options such as subtitles and sound intensity can be adjusted separately by each person.

Simultaneously Operate with Picture-in-Picture Mode

You can utilize the Picture in Picture feature to keep watching the video while using another app. This permits you to order food, check your email, or chat in the Messages application without interrupting the sound of the movie or TV show.

INVITE FRIENDS TO WATCH VIDEOS TOGETHER DURING FACETIME CALLS

Share Your Favorite Shows and Movies with Ease
On a compatible iPad, you can initiate a FaceTime conversation straight from the Apple TV application or any other supported video platforms while browsing or watching video content. SharePlay allows you to sync the video with others on the call, ensuring everyone enjoys the same experience. Every participant should have the content available on their individual device, either via a subscription or a purchase.

Steps to Share Videos Using SharePlay:

1. **Find Your Content**: Open the Apple TV application (or another supported video app) and locate the film or series you wish to share. Press on the chosen content to check the specifics.

2. **Initiate SharePlay**: Tap the SharePlay icon, then select "SharePlay."

3. **Invite Contacts**: In the "To" space, input the contacts you wish to share with, then press 'FaceTime.'

4. **Start the Call**: Once the FaceTime call is established, press 'Start' or 'Play' to commence the

use of SharePlay. The recipients will need to tap "Open" to start viewing.

Subscription Requirements

If the content requires a subscription, those who aren't subscribers will need to subscribe before they can watch.

Stream to Apple TV

After the video begins to play, you can broadcast it to your Apple TV for a larger viewing experience. For more details, see how to transmit the content you're viewing in SharePlay to your Apple TV.

ENJOY YOUR SHARED VIDEOS ON THE LARGE DISPLAY WITH APPLE TV

Seamlessly Transition from iPad to Apple TV

If you've started watching a video together on your iPad using SharePlay, you can easily send it to your Apple TV for a larger, more immersive viewing experience. Here's the process:

Steps to Send Your Video to Apple TV:

1. **From the Streaming App**: In the streaming app you're using, tap the **AirPlay** icon, then select Apple TV as the playback destination.

2. **Using Control Center**: Open Control Center on your iPad, tap the **AirPlay** icon, and choose Apple TV as the playback destination.

The video will play in sync on your Apple TV, allowing you to enjoy the big screen experience while keeping the conversation unfolding on your iPad

For more detailed instructions, refer to the "Watch together using SharePlay" section in the Apple TV User Guide.

**Share Your Favorite Tunes with your relatives
and buddies**

Listening to music together during a FaceTime call is a
fantastic way to connect with your relatives and buddies.
Whether it's an album or a favorite playlist, SharePlay
makes it easy for everyone to join in and enjoy the music
simultaneously. This is the way to do it:

Steps to Listen to Music Together:

1. **Initiate a FaceTime call**: Access the FaceTime
   application  on your iPad, as well as initiate a call
   with your friends or family.

2. **Select a Music App**: Tap the **SharePlay** icon,
   then pick an app from the "Listen and Play Together"
   section. As another option, you can navigate to the
   Home Screen and launch a music streaming

application that is compatible with SharePlay, such as the **Music** app 🎵.

3. **Choose Your Music**: Select the album or playlist you like to enjoy, then press the 'Play' button to start the music. Others on the call may need to tap "Join SharePlay" to hear the music.

Once everyone can utilize the content, the music will play simultaneously for all participants. If someone doesn't have access, they'll be prompted to get it through a subscription, purchase, or free trial if available.

Control Your Listening Experience

Each participant can use the music controls to pause, rewind, fast-forward, scrub to a different part of the song, or go to the next track. Additionally, every participant in the call has the ability to contribute songs to the communal playlist, making it a collaborative and interactive experience.

INVITE YOUR FRIENDS FOR A MUSIC LISTENING PARTY ON FACETIME

Share Your Favorite Tunes with Ease

On an iPad that meets the minimum system requirements, you can initiate a FaceTime call directly from the Music application (or any other music applications that support SharePlay) and use SharePlay to sync the music with the other participants on the call. Every participants can control the music playback and add songs to a shared queue. Here's the process:

Steps to Share Music Using SharePlay:

1) **Open the Music Application**: Launch the **Music** app 🎵 (or another supported music app) and select the music you like to share.

2) **Initiate SharePlay**:

    a) Tap ••• adjacent to the music, then select "SharePlay."

    b) Alternatively, tap ••• at the upper right, press ⬆️, then choose "SharePlay."

3) **Invite Contacts**: In the "To" space, input the contacts you wish to share with, next press 'FaceTime.'

4) **Start the Call**: Once the FaceTime call is established, press 'Start.'

To start the audio playback, the recipients should select the song title located at the upper part of the FaceTime controls, followed by pressing 'Open.' The music will start playing simultaneously for all participants in the call who possess the rights to the content.

Subscription Requirements

Every participant should have the content available on their individual device, either via a subscription or a purchase. Those who don't have access will be prompted to get it.

PLAY GAMES WITH FRIENDS IN GAME CENTER DURING FACETIME CALLS

Enjoy Multiplayer Fun with SharePlay

Playing multiplayer games together with your friends while on a FaceTime call is a fantastic way to stay connected and have fun. This is the way to set it up and start playing:

Steps to Play Games Using SharePlay:

1. **Configure Game Center:** First, set up your Game Center profile in the **Settings** app 🔘 on your iPad. Add friends to your Game Center profile.

2. **Find and Download Games**: Browse the App Store to find and download supported multiplayer games for Game Center.
3. **Initiate a FaceTime call**: When you're on a FaceTime call, access the game you want to play.
4. **Initiate SharePlay**: Tap "Start SharePlay" and adhere to the on-screen prompts to begin playing together.

Additional Features

a) **Screen Sharing**: Additionally, you can display your screen, showcasing applications, websites, and more while conversing. This is great for demonstrating gameplay or sharing other content.
b) **Apple Fitness+**: SharePlay isn't just for games. You can also work out with others using Apple Fitness+. See how to Use SharePlay to work out as a group for more details.

EFFORTLESSLY SHARE YOUR SCREEN DURING FACETIME CALLS ON IPAD

Bring Your Conversations to Life with Screen Sharing

Sharing your Screen When you are on a FaceTime call on your iPad is a fantastic way to enhance your conversations. Regardless of whether you wish to get feedback on a project, show off a photo album, or simply share a webpage, screen sharing makes it easy and interactive. This is the way to do it:

STEPS TO SHARE YOUR SCREEN:

1. **Initiate a FaceTime call**: During a call in the **FaceTime** application on your iPad, press the screen to reveal the FaceTime options if they aren't already visible.
2. **Initiate Screen Sharing**: Tap the **SharePlay** icon , then select "Share My Screen."

A descending sequence from 3 to 1 will be displayed, followed by a miniature representation of your screen will be visible within the FaceTime call. Other participants in the call have the option to select this image to magnify it and view your content in detail.

End screen sharing.

To End screen sharing, simply tap the **SharePlay** icon again.

EFFORTLESS COLLABORATION ON DOCUMENTS USING FACETIME ON IPAD

Unlock Seamless Teamwork with FaceTime
Collaborating on a document during a FaceTime call on your iPad is simpler than you might think. Whether you're a novice, a senior, a teenager, a parent, or a professional, this manual will guide you step-by-step through the procedure step-by-step. Embrace the ease of learning and enjoy the positive experience of working together in real-time.

HOW TO JOINTLY WORK ON A DOCUMENT

1. **Start Your FaceTime Call:** Begin by initiating a FaceTime conversation with the individuals you wish

to work jointly with. If you're unsure how to start a call, refer to the FaceTime app's instructions on making a call.

2. **Access Collaboration Tools:** During the call, touch the screen to display the FaceTime controls. Look for the collaboration Symbol (typically depicted as a symbol like this:). If it doesn't appear right away, tap the screen to reveal the controls.

3. **Open Your Document**: Find the file you want to co-edit. Open it, and then hit the collaboration icon again to start the sharing process.

4. **Share the Document:** Select your preferred method for disseminating the document with your collaborators. You can use FaceTime, Mail, AirDrop, or Messages. Once shared, tap the "Collaborate" button .

5. **Notify Your Collaborators:** Your collaborators will receive an alert indicating your successful share of a document for collaboration. They can select to either affirm or deny the invitation. Those who accept will have the document open on their device.

6. **Collaborate in Real-Time:** Tap "Collaborate" at the upper part of your display. Now, everyone who has accepted the invitation can modify the document and see updates made by others in real-time.

MASTERING VIDEO CONFERENCING FEATURES ON YOUR IPAD

Elevate Your Video Calls with Fun and Functional Effects

Video conferencing has become a vital part of our daily lives, whether you're catching up with friends, collaborating with colleagues, or attending virtual meetings. With your iPad, you can enhance your video calls by using exciting video effects and interactive reactions. Let's explore how you can optimize the use of these features with ease!

UNLOCKING VIDEO EFFECTS DURING YOUR CALL

In case you're in a video call—whether it's through the FaceTime app or a third-party video conferencing app—Just adhere to these easy steps to add a touch of magic to your conversation:

1) **Access Control Center**: Start by opening Control Center during your video conference call. This is done by swiping downward from the upper-right corner of your display.

2) **Choose Your Video Effects**: Hit the "Video Effects" option and explore the following features to enhance your video call:

   a) **Center Stage**: This feature keeps you and anyone else in the frame as you move around. It's perfect for dynamic calls where you're on the move or interacting with others. (Available on supported iPad models.) Learn how to activate Center Stage for a more engaging call.

   b) **Portrait Mode**: Blur your background to keep the aim on you. This mode automatically blurs the background, making you the star of the show. Adjust the blur level by tapping the control button . Discover how to fine-tune your background blur for a more professional look.

c) **Studio Light**: Illuminate your face while dimming the background. This effect makes you stand out in any lighting condition. Modify the light intensity by tapping the control button ⬤ for the perfect brightness. Find out how to generate a well-lit, polished appearance on camera.

d) **Reactions**: Add a personal touch by using hand gestures to trigger reactions during your call. If you prefer, you may also press the icons that appear when you touch and hold your video tile in the call. Explore how to activate and use reactions to make your video calls more interactive.

ADDING REACTIONS TO YOUR VIDEO CALLS: MAKE YOUR CONVERSATIONS FUN AND ENGAGING

Bring Your Video Calls to Life with Interactive Reactions

Video calls don't have to be just about talking; they can be fun and interactive too! With your iPad, you can add playful and dynamic reactions to your calls, making your virtual conversations more lively and engaging. Whether you're using the FaceTime or any other video calling application, you can enhance your calls with 3D augmented reality effects. This is the way to bring a burst of excitement to your video calls!

How to Add Reactions During a Call

1) **Enable Hand Gestures**: First, make sure that hand gestures for reactions are turned on. Open Control Center by swiping downward from the

upper-right corner of your display. Tap on "Video Effects" and ensure that "Reactions" is activated.

2) **Use Gestures for Reactions**: During your call, Position your hands off your face and take a moment briefly to activate the desired reaction. Your iPad will recognize the gesture and fill the camera frame with a fun, 3D effect. Here's a quick guide to the reactions you can use:

a) **Hearts** : Show some love with hearts .

b) **Thumbs-up** : Give a positive affirmation with a thumbs-up .

c) **Thumbs-down** : Express disagreement with a thumbs-down .

d) **Balloons** : Celebrate with a burst of colorful balloons .

e) **Rain** : Add a whimsical touch with a rain effect .

f) **Confetti** : Mark a special moment with a shower of confetti .

g) **Laser Burst** : Surprise with a dynamic laser burst .

h) **Fireworks** : Celebrate achievements with a dazzling fireworks display .

3) **Tap to React**: If you prefer, you can also infuse reactions by touching and holding your video tile

288

during the call. Icons for reactions will appear; simply tap the one you want to use.

SEAMLESSLY TRANSFER YOUR FACETIME CALL FROM IPAD TO ANY APPLE DEVICE

Effortlessly Shift Your Call to Stay Connected Wherever You Are

Imagine you're in the middle of an important FaceTime call on your iPad, as well as need to switch to another device. Whether it's moving the call to your iPhone or Mac, or even using your iPad as a webcam for FaceTime on your MacBook or Apple TV, the process is straightforward and intuitive. This is the way to make the transition smoothly and keep your conversations going without a hitch.

HOW TO SWITCH A FACETIME CALL FROM YOUR IPAD

If you're using your iPad for a FaceTime call and want to switch to a different Apple gadget, like your iPhone or MacBook, follow these easy steps. Ensure your devices are running macOS 13, iOS 16, or iPadOS 16 or later, and that you're logged in with the identical Apple ID on all devices.

1) **Prepare Your Devices**: Verify that both your iPad and the device you want to hand off to (iPhone or Mac) are logged in utilizing identical Apple ID and are updated to the required software versions.

2) **Initiate the Hand Off**: While you're on the FaceTime call on your iPad, look at the device you

want to switch to. You'll see a notification suggesting "Move call to this [device]." Tap on this notification to transfer the call.

3) **Alternative Method**: On your other device, you may also press the FaceTime icon on the screen's upper side. This will display a sneak peek of the call, exhibiting your camera, microphone, and audio configurations, and allowing you to continue the call on that device.

4) **Adjust Settings as Needed**: After initiating the handoff, a preview of your call will appear, allowing you to adjust camera and microphone settings if needed.

5) **Confirm and Adjust**: A preview of your call will appear on the target device, showing camera and audio settings. Make sure these settings are as you want them, then tap "Switch" or "Join" to finalize the handoff. The call will now continue on the new device.

6) **Return Option**: On your original device, a banner will appear confirming that the call has been moved. You'll see a "Switch" button, which you can tap if you like to bring the call back to the iPad.

TRANSFERRING YOUR FACETIME CALL FROM IPAD TO APPLE TV 4K

For an even larger screen experience, you can switch your FaceTime call from your iPad to an Apple TV 4K (from the 2nd generation onwards), using your iPad as the webcam and microphone:

1. **Prepare Your Devices**: Ensure both your iPad and Apple TV 4K are logged in utilizing identical Apple ID

and that your iPad is a supported model for Continuity Camera.

2. **Start or Receive the Call**: Begin or answer the FaceTime call on your iPad.

3. **Hand Off to Apple TV 4K**: Follow the instructions for transferring the call to Apple TV 4K. Once the call is moved, your iPad will serve as a webcam and microphone, and the call will continue on the larger screen of the Apple TV.

4. **Consult Apple's Guide**: For detailed steps on how to complete the handoff and use FaceTime on Apple TV 4K, refer to the specific instructions provided for this model.

MASTERING FACETIME VIDEO SETTINGS ON YOUR IPAD

Effortlessly Customize Your Video Call Experience

When using FaceTime on your iPad, you have several video settings within easy reach that can enhance your call experience. Regardless of whether you wish to brighten your video, adjust the framing, or switch your camera, it's easy to tailor your video settings to fit your needs. Here's a straightforward guide to help you make these adjustments effortlessly.

HOW TO ADJUST YOUR FACETIME VIDEO SETTINGS

1) **Turn On Center Stage**: Center Stage is a fantastic feature available on supported iPad models that

automatically keeps you centered in the frame as you move around during a call.

a) **Activate Center Stage**: When you are on a FaceTime call, glide down from the upper-right section of your screen to open Control Center.

b) **Enable the Feature**: Tap "Video Effects" and then tap "Center Stage" to turn it on. If you like to turn Center Stage off, simply tap it again.

c) **Alternative Access**: On some iPad models, you might see the **Center Stage** icon directly on your video tile. You may also press your video tile and then hit the **Center Stage** icon to activate the feature.

ACHIEVING A BLURRED BACKGROUND EFFECT IN PORTRAIT MODE

Portrait Mode is perfect for making sure the focus stays on you by automatically blurring the background during your FaceTime calls. Here's how to activate it:

1) **Switch to Portrait Mode During a Call:**

a) When you are on a FaceTime call, press your video tile to bring up additional options.

b) Tap the Portrait Mode Symbol (typically depicted as a portrait frame) on your tile to enable the feature. If you like to turn it off, just tap the icon again.

2) **Alternative Method Using Control Center**:

a) Pull down from the upper-right corner to access Control Center.

b) Tap "Video Effects," and then select the Portrait Mode option to turn it on or off.

Portrait Mode helps create a professional look by keeping you sharp and in focus while blurring everything behind you, just like in the Camera app's Portrait mode.

HOW TO HIGHLIGHT YOUR FACE WITH STUDIO LIGHT

Studio Light is another fantastic feature that brightens your face while dimming the background, making you stand out during your video calls. Here's the process to utilize it:

1) **Activate Studio Light During a Call**:
   a) Open Control Center by swiping downward from the upper-right corner of your display.
   b) Tap "Video Effects," and then select the **Studio Light** icon to turn it on. If you like to turn it off, just tap the icon again.
2) **Alternative Access**:
   a) When you are on a FaceTime call, you may also press your video tile to access the Studio Light option directly. Tap the icon to adjust the lighting as needed.

HOW TO TRANSITION TO THE REAR CAMERA

Sometimes, you might like to show something behind you while engaged in a FaceTime call. Switching to the rear camera is easy:

1) **Transition to the Rear Camera**:
   a) When you are on a FaceTime call, press your video tile to reveal additional controls.
   b) Tap the rear camera symbol (typically depicted as a camera switch symbol) to Transition to the Rear Camera.

2) **Return to the Front Camera**:
   a) To switch back to the front camera, simply tap the same icon again.
3) **Adjust Image Size**:
   a) When using the rear camera, you can enlarge the image by tapping the zoom icon (often marked as 1x). Tapping it again will return the image to its normal size.

HOW TO SWITCH OFF YOUR CAMERA

In case you need to switch off your camera during a call—perhaps for privacy or to save bandwidth—follow these steps:

1) **Switch Off the Camera**:
   a) During your FaceTime call, press the screen to reveal the call controls.

   b) Hit the camera symbol to turn off your video feed. Hit it once more to reactivate the camera.

ENHANCE YOUR FACETIME EXPERIENCE: MASTERING AUDIO SETTINGS ON YOUR IPAD

Transform Your Calls with Spatial Audio

FaceTime audio configurations on your iPad offer incredible features that can elevate your calling experience. One standout feature is **Spatial Audio**, which creates a more immersive sound environment, making it feel as though your friends are by your side. Their voices are not just clear but also positioned spatially, mimicking the direction they display on your screen. This feature is available on supported iPad models and works seamlessly with AirPods (3rd generation), AirPods Pro (all models), and AirPods Max.

FOCUS ON YOUR VOICE: FILTERING OUT BACKGROUND NOISE

For those moments when you want to confirm that your voice is the star of the conversation, FaceTime has you covered with the **Voice Isolation** mode. This setting is perfect for situations where you need to eliminate background noises and make sure that your voice comes through loud and clear. To activate this feature, simply open the Control Center during your FaceTime call, tap on **Mic Mode**, and select **Voice Isolation**. This easy adjustment will prioritize your voice, ensuring a clearer and more focused communication experience.

MASTERING FACETIME AUDIO: CUSTOMIZE YOUR SOUND SETTINGS ON IPAD

Embrace the Full Audio Experience with Wide Spectrum Mode

The **Wide Spectrum** mode lets you capture not only your voice but also the ambient noise while you are on a FaceTime call. This feature ensures that both your voice and the ambient sounds are transmitted clearly, making your conversations more vibrant and engaging. To activate Wide Spectrum mode, open Control Center during your call, tap on **Mic Mode**, and then select **Wide Spectrum**. This setting is available on supported iPad models and permits you to share a richer audio experience with your callers.

CONTROL YOUR AUDIO: TURNING SOUND ON AND OFF

Managing the sound during your FaceTime calls is straightforward. In case you need to silence the audio, just touch the screen to reveal the FaceTime controls (if they're not already visible), then tap the **sound icon** to switch off the sound. To reactivate it, just press the button once more. When the sound is off, your microphone will still pick up your voice, and you'll see a notification indicating that your mic is muted. To unmute, just tap the sound icon again, and you're back in action.

TRANSFORM YOUR LOOK: CHANGING YOUR VISUAL PRESENTATION DURING A FACETIME CALL ON IPAD

Express Yourself with Memojis and Fun Filters

Elevate your FaceTime calls with a personal touch by changing your appearance directly in the app. Regardless of whether you wish to become your favorite Memoji or add a splash of creativity with built-in filters, it's all at your fingertips. This is the way to effortlessly switch up your look and make your calls more engaging.

BECOME A MEMOJI: YOUR DIGITAL DOPPELGÄNGER

If you have an iPad integrated with a TrueDepth camera, you can bring your Memoji to life during your FaceTime calls. This feature Records your gestures, facial reactions, and vocal tones, turning them into a digital character that mirrors your actions—even if you stick out your tongue! To start using a Memoji, Just adhere to these easy steps:

1. **During a FaceTime Call:** Tap your video tile to reveal more options. In case you don't find the options, tap the screen to make them appear.

2. **Select Your Memoji:** Touch the **Effects** control (symbolized by a star), then choose the **Memoji** option. Swipe through the available characters and select the one you want to use.

With your chosen Memoji, the other caller will hear your voice while seeing your Memoji performing your expressions and movements, adding a fun and personal touch to your conversation.

USE FILTERS TO REFRESH YOUR APPEARANCE

Adding a filter during your FaceTime call is straightforward yet effective way to change your look and make your video chats more dynamic. This is the way to use filters to transform your appearance:

1. **Activate Filters:** When you are on a FaceTime call, press your video tile to bring up additional options. Next, press the **Effects** button (represented by a star) if you're using a supported model.

2. **Select a Filter:** Tap **Filters** to open the filter options. Swipe left or right to preview different filters, then hit the one you'd like to use.

Filters can give your FaceTime calls a fresh, fun, or polished look, making it easy to adapt your appearance to match the mood or setting.

ADD A TEXT LABEL FOR EXTRA FLAIR

Text labels can add a touch of personality or provide useful information during your FaceTime calls. Here's how to include a text label in your video:

1. **Show Controls:** During your call, tap the screen to reveal the FaceTime controls. Next, press the **Effects** button (star icon) to access more options.

2. **Add a Label:** Tap **Text** Aa to select a text label. To see additional label styles, swipe up from the upper section of the text window.

3. **Customize Your Text:** Once the label is selected, type in the text you want to display. Tap away from the text field to finalize it.

4. **Position the Label:** Drag the label to your desired location on the screen.

To remove the label, tap it and then hit the **Delete** button (trash can icon).

SPICE UP YOUR CALL WITH STICKERS

Adding stickers is a fun way to personalize your FaceTime calls and express yourself creatively. This is the way to easily include stickers in your video:

1) **Access Stickers:** During your call, press the screen to reveal the FaceTime controls. Tap the **Effects** button (star icon), then:

   a) Tap the **Memoji Stickers** button to infuse a Memoji sticker.

   b) Tap the **Emoji Stickers** button to select an Emoji sticker.

c) Alternatively, tap **Aa**, swipe up, and tap the **Stickers** option ☺.

2) **Add and Position a Sticker:** Tap on a sticker to include it to your call. Swipe left to explore more sticker options.

3) **Move and Delete:** Drag the sticker to your preferred location on the screen. To remove a sticker, tap it and then hit the **Delete** button ⊗ (trash can icon).

Stickers add a playful touch to your conversations and help convey your emotions or just add some fun.

INCORPORATE SHAPES FOR ADDED CREATIVITY

Shapes can be used to highlight information or simply add a creative element to your FaceTime calls. Adhere to these instructions to include shapes:

1. **Add Shapes:** During your call, tap your video tile to reveal additional options, then tap the **Effects** button ✪ (star icon).

2. **Select a Shape:** Tap **Shapes** 〰 and choose a shape to include to your call. To view more shape options, glide your finger upwards starting from the upper section of the shapes panel.

3. **Position and Remove:** Drag the shape to the desired location on the screen. To delete a shape, tap it and then hit the **Delete** button ⊗ (trash can icon).

SEAMLESSLY TRANSITION: LEAVING A FACETIME CALL OR SWITCHING TO MESSAGES ON IPAD

EXIT A FACETIME CALL WITH EASE

If you have to terminate a FaceTime call, the process is quick and straightforward. This is the way to end a call at any moment:

1. **Display the Controls:** Hit the display to reveal the FaceTime settings. If the controls are not already visible, this simple tap will make them appear.

2. **End the Call:** Tap the red **End Call** button (represented by a red phone icon) to exit the call.

This intuitive method validates that you can exit the call without any hassle, making it easy to manage your FaceTime conversations.

SWITCH TO MESSAGES FOR ONGOING CONVERSATIONS

If you'd rather to continue your chat in the Messages application, you can seamlessly transition from FaceTime. Here's how to switch to a Messages conversation:

1. **Reveal the Controls:** During your FaceTime call, Press on the display to reveal the FaceTime options.

2. **Switch to Messages:** Tap the **Info** button (an "i" in a circle) at the peak of the controls, then select **Messages**.

This feature allows you to easily jump to a Messages thread that includes everyone on the call, keeping the conversation going in a text format.

KEEP UNWANTED FACETIME CALLERS AT BAY WITH EASE

Effortlessly Block Unwanted FaceTime Calls and Group Calls

Dealing with unwanted FaceTime calls can be frustrating, but blocking these interruptions is simple and straightforward. Whether it's a one-to-one FaceTime call or a Group FaceTime session, you have the power to control who can reach you. This guide will lead you through the steps to block unwanted callers and help you regain control over your FaceTime experience.

BLOCKING INDIVIDUAL FACETIME CONVERSATIONS FROM UNDESIRED CALLERS

If you encounter an undesired FaceTime call, follow these easy steps to block the caller (this feature is available in iPadOS 17.4 and later):

1) **Block During or After the Call:**
   a) **When you are on a FaceTime call:** Simply tap the ⓘ icon next to the call and select "Block Caller."
   b) **From Your FaceTime Call History:** Locate the call you want to block, tap the ✋ icon adjacent to it, and choose "Block Caller."
   c) **Using the Recents List in the Phone App on Your iPhone:** Slide left on the call you wish to block, then hit the "Block" icon.

2) **Confirm the Block:**
   a) Tap "Block" to finalize the action.
To unblock a contact later, find their name, mobile number, or email in your call log. Tap the ⓘ icon next to their contact details, scroll down, and pick "Unblock Caller."

Handling Calls from Unknown Numbers
When you end a call from an unknown number and see a "Call Ended" screen, you have a couple of options:

a) **Block Caller:** Tap "Block Caller" to prevent any further contact from that number.

b) **Create Contact:** If you'd like to add the caller to your contacts, tap "Create Contact."

Choosing to block the caller will also give you the option to report the call as spam, which helps improve your overall experience.

EFFORTLESSLY MANAGE GROUP FACETIME CALLS AND SILENCE UNWANTED CALLERS

Block Unwanted Group FaceTime Calls and Mute Incoming Calls from Unrecognized Numbers with Simple Steps
Group FaceTime calls can sometimes include unwanted participants, while unknown callers might disrupt your peace. Luckily, with iPadOS 17.5 and later, you have powerful tools to manage these situations. This is the way to handle unwanted group calls and ensure your FaceTime experience remains smooth and interruption-free.

Blocking All Participants in Group FaceTime Calls

If you find yourself in an unwanted Group FaceTime call with unknown participants, you can block everyone involved by adhering to these straightforward instructions:

1) **Block During the Call Ringing:**
   a) While the call is ringing, tap the left side of the notification to expand the window.
   b) Tap the (i) icon on the screen's upper side.
   c) Select "Block All Participants" to prevent further communication.

2) **Block During an Ongoing Group FaceTime Call:**
   a) During the call, press the (i) symbol at the Screen's Base.
   b) Choose "Block All Participants" to stop all members from contacting you.

3) **Block After the Call Ends:**
   a) Navigate to your FaceTime call history.
   b) Slide left on the Group FaceTime call you like to block.
   c) Tap the "Block" icon 🤚, then select "Block All Participants."

Please Note: The option to block all participants is not available if any participant is in your contacts list.

Silencing FaceTime Calls from Unknown Callers

To avoid disruptions from unknown callers, you can easily silence these calls:

1) **Access the Settings:**

a) Launch the **Settings** application on your iPad.
b) Navigate to **FaceTime**.
2) **Activate Mute for Unrecognized Callers:**
   a) Switch on the 'Mute Unrecognized Callers' feature.

With this feature activated, FaceTime calls originating from numbers not registered within your contact directory, numbers you haven't called before, or numbers not suggested by Siri will be silenced. These calls will go to voicemail and be listed in your Recents list for your review.

EASILY REPORT UNWANTED FACETIME CALLS AS SPAM ON YOUR IPAD

Keep Your FaceTime Experience Secure: Simple Steps to Report Spam Calls

Receiving unwanted FaceTime calls from unknown or bothersome numbers can be frustrating. Fortunately, you can take control and ensure these calls don't disturb you again. With iPadOS 17.1 and later, Apple provides an easy way to report these calls as spam. This is the way to handle it:

REPORTING AN INDIVIDUAL FACETIME CALL AS SPAM

Upon receiving an undesired FaceTime call, you can both block the caller and report them as spam. Just adhere to these easy steps to maintain your peace of mind:
1) **From Your FaceTime Call History:**
   a) Open your FaceTime call history.

b) Slide left on the call you like to report.

c) Tap the "Report Junk" button ✋.

d) Confirm by tapping "Block and Report Junk."

2) **During or After a FaceTime Call:**

a) While on a call or in your FaceTime call history, find the caller's name, mobile number, or email.

b) Tap the ⓘ icon next to their details.

c) Select "Block Caller."

d) Then choose "Block and Report Junk" to report the call as spam and block further communication.

EFFICIENTLY REPORT GROUP FACETIME CALLS AS SPAM ON YOUR IPAD

Take Charge of Group FaceTime Calls: Simple Steps to Block and Report Spam

Handling unwanted Group FaceTime calls from unknown participants can be challenging, but with iPadOS 17.5 and later, you have powerful tools to manage these interruptions. Here's a straightforward guide to help you block and report spam calls effectively.

Reporting a Group FaceTime Call as Spam

If you receive a Group FaceTime call with unknown participants and want to block them and report the call as spam, follow these easy steps:

1) **During the Group FaceTime Call:**

a) While the call is active, press the ⓘ symbol at the Screen's Base.

b) Select "Block All Participants" to prevent further communication from everyone in the call.

2) **After the Group FaceTime Call Ends:**

a) Open your FaceTime call history.
b) Slide left on the call you like to report.
c) Tap the "Block" icon , then select "Block All Participants."

Note: If any participant in the Group FaceTime call is within your contacts directory, you won't see the "Block All Participants" option.

Additional Tip: To avoid undesired FaceTime calls linked to your mobile number, navigate to 'Settings > press FaceTime' on your iPad. Uncheck your phone number in the "You Can Be Reached by FaceTime At" section. You will still receive FaceTime calls linked to your Apple ID if it remains selected.

INDEX

T